COLLINS LIVING HISTORY

The French Revolution and Napoleon

Fiona Macdonald

Series editor: Christopher Culpin

Contents

attainment target 1

Questions aimed at this attainment target find out how much you know and understand about the past. Some questions are about how things were different in history: not only people's food, or clothes but their beliefs too. Others are about how things change through history, sometimes quickly, sometimes slowly, sometimes a little, sometimes a lot. Other questions ask you to explain why things were different in the past, and why changes took place.

attainment target 2

This attainment target is about understanding what people say about the past. Historians, as well as lots of other people, try to describe what the past was like. Sometimes they say different things. This attainment target is about understanding these differences and why they occur.

attainment target 3

This attainment target is about historical sources and how we use them to find out about the past. Some questions are about the historical evidence we can get from sources. Others ask you about how valuable this evidence might be.

Introduction

In 1789, the inhabitants of Paris, the capital city of France, went on the rampage. They set fire to a big royal prison, and murdered the governor and guards. A few weeks later, an angry crowd attacked the royal palace, and captured the King and Queen. Meanwhile, French politicians staged a 'sit-in', and drew up a 'Declaration of the Rights of Man'. In the countryside, mobs attacked tax collectors, and besieged stately homes.

What was happening to France – the most 'civilised' nation in eighteenth century Europe? Why were the French people so rebellious? What were their complaints? Was all the violence necessary? And what on earth would happen next? This book looks at the dramatic events of 1789 and the 10 years that followed, and discusses why they took place. It also explains what happened after revolutionary leaders lost control of the country, and let a daring young army officer, called Napoleon Bonaparte, seize power in 1799.

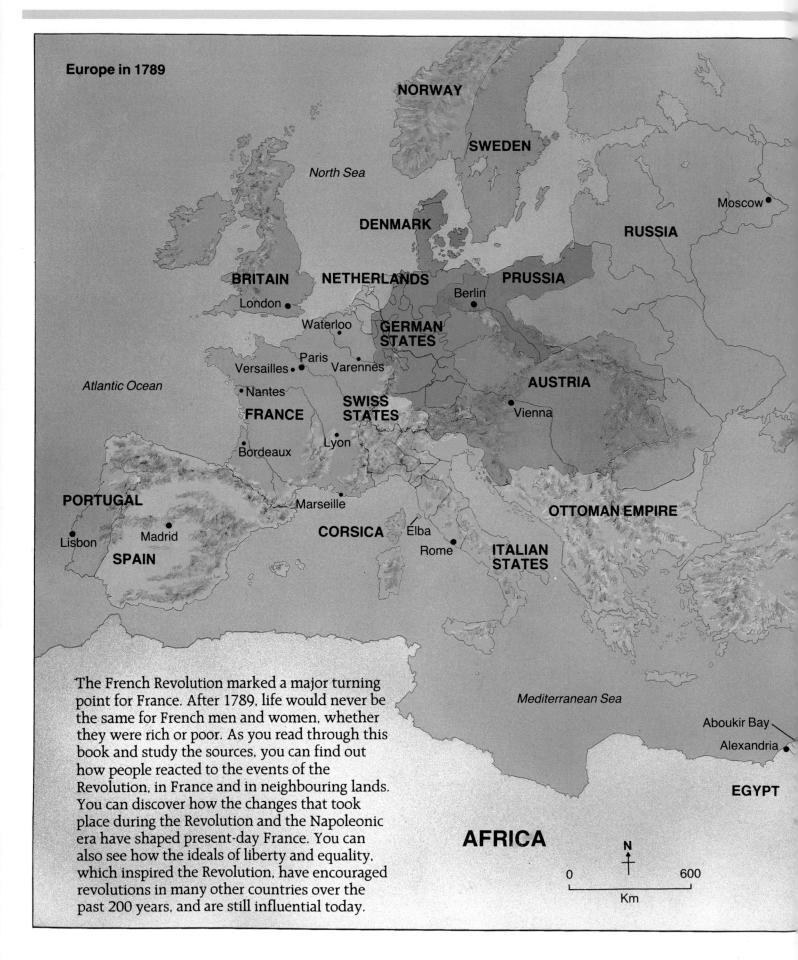

Europe in 1789

NORWAY

SWEDEN

North Sea

DENMARK

RUSSIA
• Moscow

BRITAIN
• London

NETHERLANDS

PRUSSIA
Berlin •

GERMAN
STATES

Waterloo •

Atlantic Ocean

Paris
Versailles • • • Varennes

• Nantes

SWISS
STATES

AUSTRIA
• Vienna

FRANCE

• Bordeaux

Lyon •

Marseille •

PORTUGAL

Lisbon •

Madrid •

SPAIN

CORSICA

Élba •

Rome •

ITALIAN
STATES

OTTOMAN EMPIRE

Mediterranean Sea

Aboukir Bay

Alexandria •

EGYPT

AFRICA

N

0   600
Km

The French Revolution marked a major turning
point for France. After 1789, life would never be
the same for French men and women, whether
they were rich or poor. As you read through this
book and study the sources, you can find out
how people reacted to the events of the
Revolution, in France and in neighbouring lands.
You can discover how the changes that took
place during the Revolution and the Napoleonic
era have shaped present-day France. You can
also see how the ideals of liberty and equality,
which inspired the Revolution, have encouraged
revolutions in many other countries over the
past 200 years, and are still influential today.

Black Sea

● Jaffa

ANCIEN REGIME (royal rule)	**1780**	
	1787	Financial crisis, widespread discontent.
	1788	Bad harvests and food shortages. Decision to call Estates-General.
	1789	Famine and riots. Attack on the Bastille by mobs. The Revolution begins. Declaration of the Rights of Man and the Citizen.
REVOLUTIONARY ASSEMBLIES	**1791**	The royal family tries to escape.
	1792	Monarchy abolished. A republic declared.
	1793	Louis XVI executed. Jacobin faction seizes power. Terror begins.
THE TERROR	**1794**	Robespierre executed – the end of the Terror.
THE DIRECTORY	**1795**	Directory (committee of moderate politicians) now rules France.
	1796	Napoleon's first victories in battle.
NAPOLEON'S RULE	**1799**	Napoleon seizes power.

	1804	Napoleon becomes Emperor
		    – reforms French government.
		    – starts to conquer vast empire.

	1812	Napoleon defeated in Russia.
NEW MONARCHY	**1814**	Louis XVIII becomes king.
	1815	France defeated at battle of Waterloo. Napoleon sent into exile. France governed by a King again.
	1821	Napoleon dies in exile.

Land and people

France in the 18th century

Eighteenth century France was a big country compared with other countries in Europe. As you can see from Source 1, the French government ruled over an area twice the size of England and Wales, and almost ten times the size of Switzerland.

In the early 18th century, there were around 20 million French people. However, by the time the French Revolution began in 1789, there were probably at least 26 million.

France was made up of what had been small, independent nations. These had been brought under French control during the 15th and 16th centuries. French peasants therefore spoke different local languages, lived in different styles of houses, and grew different kinds of crops. They even had different faiths: most were Catholics, but some were Protestants. Their daily lives were governed by a confusing number of ancient local laws.

AIMS

In this unit, we look at France in the years before the outbreak of the French Revolution, from around AD 1770 to 1789. We learn how French society was organised, how the economy was run and how the country was governed. What was life like for the people of France at this time?

As we study pre-revolutionary France, can we see any conflicts or tensions within society that might help us to suggest why the Revolution broke out?

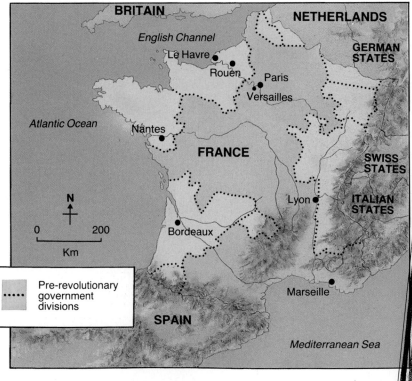

SOURCE 2
How one 18th century French artist saw peasant life. The original caption reads 'Born for hard work and suffering.'

SOURCE 1
France in the 18th century.

SOURCE 3
Traditional farmland in Central France today.

> 'All the country girls and women are without shoes and stockings; and the ploughmen at work have neither *sabots* (clogs) nor stockings to their feet. This is a poverty that strikes at the root of national prosperity.'

SOURCE 4
Written by Arthur Young, an English traveller in France, 10 June 1787.

Peasants

Almost all of these people were peasants earning a living from the land, but this did not make them equal. Their income varied greatly, depending on how much land they farmed, and who it belonged to (see Source 3).

The wealthiest peasants were called LABOUREURS. They owned or rented large farms, and produced enough food to feed their families and still have a surplus to sell. Next came MÉTAYERS who leased fields from landlords, and were provided with tools, seeds and livestock. In return, the *métayers* gave the landlords at least half of what they produced every year. The rest struggled to feed their families from the land they rented. Often, they had to take on other work to make extra money, or leave their homes for part of the year to search for work in the towns. Others became beggars.

Poverty and taxes

Almost all these peasants, except the *laboureurs*, were extremely poor (see Sources 2 and 4). Their hardships were increased by the taxes they had to pay. Unlike other groups in society they had not found a way of avoiding them.

1 Although many peasants were poor, they did not protest or rebel. Suggest two reasons for this.

2 If you were a peasant who wanted to improve your life, what would you do?

The typical tax bill of a peasant family each year might include:
- *taille personelle* – a yearly tax on possessions
- *capitation* – poll tax
- *vingtième* – a tax of one-twentieth on land
- tithe – a tax on produce, paid to the Church

Almost everyone in France also paid:
- *gabelle* – a tax on salt
- *douanes* – customs duties on goods moved to market.

Peasants also had to pay ancient FEUDAL DUES such as paying the local lord to use his mill to grind their corn, or his oven to bake their bread. By the 18th century, the nobles who had inherited the rights to collect these dues had usually 'sold' them to wealthy businessmen or to *laboureurs*. It was always the poor peasants who ended up paying, as Source 5 shows.

SOURCE 5
Pre-revolutionary cartoon, complaining about the burden of taxation carried by the peasants.

Nobles, bourgeoisie and clergy

Peasants made up the largest section of French society – about 80 per cent. We can divide the others into three separate groups: nobles, bourgeois and clergy.

The nobles

Traditionally, nobles were identified as men and women with titles – dukes, duchesses etc – who had noble ANCESTORS. They could trace their families back for many generations, to men who fought alongside kings in far-off medieval times.

By the 18th century, this ancient definition of nobility was very out of date. Many of the old noble families had died out, or had lost their wealth and influence (see Source 6). Their place had been taken by men who had been given lands and a title as a reward for government service – acting as royal ministers – or for duties in the local *parlements* (law courts), which played an important part in French political life. These 'new' nobles were often lawyers. The divisions between 'old' and 'new' nobles were gradually dying out. All that mattered was riches, a title, and political power. Nobles who had achieved these things built magnificent stately homes and commemorated their success in elegant family portraits, like the group in Source 7.

The bourgeoisie

'Bourgeoisie' means 'town-dwellers'. The bourgeoisie in 18th century France was made up of merchants, craft-workers, factory-owners, doctors, teachers, journalists, writers and artists. There were lawyers, who worked as government officials, and a great many shopkeepers. There were also servants, unemployed peasants (see Source 8) and beggars.

Trade and prosperity

French towns prospered during the 18th century. Successful members of the bourgeoisie had plenty of money, earned through trade, from government positions, or in professional fees. Nobles, bourgeoisie and clergy played an important part in government (see Source 9). They also spent a lot of money on enjoying themselves (see Source 10).

'They allow their country houses to go to decay . . . and reside in dark holes in the Upper Town . . . without light, air or convenience. There they starve within doors, that they may have the wherewithall to purchase fine clothes and appear (in public) dressed once a day . . .'

SOURCE 6
Description of impoverished nobles' lifestyle written by an Irishman, Tobias Smollett, in 1763.

SOURCE 8
Political cartoon: 'The awakening of the Third Estate', showing a nobleman, a priest and a peasant all in ceremonial dress.

SOURCE 7
Not all nobles were as wealthy as the Duc de Penthièvres, shown here with his wife and family.

KING

- head of state – in charge of policy for war and peace

- made new laws and was chief judge

- appointed national and local government officials

- raised taxes and controlled currency

- had duty to:
  – uphold privileges of PARLEMENTS
  – respect the law
  – summon ESTATES-GENERAL to raise new taxes

PARLEMENTS

- ancient local law courts – tried criminals

- members: nobles and well-educated bourgeois

- debated and accepted all new royal laws

- could be overruled by KING

- often quarrelled with KING

ESTATES-GENERAL

- assembly of representatives elected by:
  1st Estate – clergy
  2nd Estate – nobles
  3rd Estate – everyone else

- expressed public opinion

- authorised new taxes when KING asked for them

- had not met since 1614

SOURCE 9
Structure of the French government before the Revolution.

SOURCE 10
Wealthy bourgeois men and women met to walk and talk at public promenades like the Gallery of the Palais Royal, seen here.

These wealthy town-dwellers were usually ambitious. Often, they were richer than the old aristocrats. Arranged marriages between poor noble sons and rich bourgeois daughters were common. Both families would hope to benefit from the deal. As one historian said, 'Not all nobles . . . were rich, but, sooner or later, all the rich ended up noble.'

The clergy

Parish priests played an important part in society, especially in the countryside. Apart from their religious duties, they were often the only educated people in villages, so they sometimes acted as leaders of political opinion as well. Monasteries were also powerful, because they were major landowners. The Church owned 20 per cent of all the land in France. Senior churchmen, such as bishops and abbots, took part in national and international politics. They were often appointed from noble families, and were chosen for their high status and good political connections, rather than their holy lives. You can see one of these 'noble' churchmen, dressed in splendid robes, next to the nobleman in Source 8.

1 Look at Sources 7, 8 and 10. Can you tell, just from these pictures, who was the richest person?

2 Which would you rather have been, a noble, a bourgeois, or a priest?

SOURCE 11
Portrait of King Louis XVI, by Antoine-François Callet (1741–1823).

'He is honest and wishes to do good, but has neither genius (intelligence) or education to show the way towards that good which he desires.'

SOURCE 12
Comment by the American ambassador to Louis XVI's court.

'It is in my person alone that sovereign power lives ... It is from me alone that my courts get their authority ... It is to me alone that law-making power belongs ... The whole public order comes from me, ...'

SOURCE 13
Remark made by Louis XV.

SOURCE 14
The royal palace at Versailles, near Paris, where Louis XVI and his family lived. It was the centre of royal government.

Kings and courtiers

King Louis XVI of France came to the throne in 1774, when he was 20 years old. He was a member of the Bourbon DYNASTY which had ruled France since 1589. Source 11 shows a splendid portrait of Louis XVI. The artist has copied the majestic pose and the costume from an earlier portrait of Louis XIV (Louis XVI's great-great grandfather). Louis XVI tried to follow the example set by his glorious ancestor, but found it very difficult indeed.

King Louis XIV had been intelligent, ruthless and determined. Louis XVI was different (see Source 12). He was well-meaning, but shy and not very quick-thinking. Hunting and horse-riding were his great passions. He preferred talking to his grooms (workers in the stables) than to his ministers. He did not know how to handle crafty, ambitious politicians.

A Divine Right to rule?

King Louis XIV believed that God had given him the right to rule. Therefore, his subjects, the French people, should obey him without question. Source 13 shows that later kings followed his example. Louis XVI was brought up to believe in Divine Right too. According to this theory, kings ruled with the help of a parliament, called the Estates-General, but this had not met since 1614. Ever since then, kings had governed the country with the help of ministers chosen by themselves.

Many people in France were unhappy with this system of government. The nobles – especially those who served as judges in the local *parlements* – wanted to limit royal power by bringing back their traditional rights. The bourgeoisie felt frustrated by royal government, which was often slow, inefficient and CORRUPT.

SOURCE 16

A 'galante' (elegant, refined and romantic) painting by Antoine Watteau (1684–1721), showing an imaginary party in an enchanted landscape.

SOURCE 15

Comment by the Swedish nobleman Axel von Fersen, a great friend of Marie Antoinette.

We are in a tumult of feasts, delights and all manner of entertainments. . . We never have time to do all arranged for us . . . We have already had a grand opera at Versailles and a State Ball, not to mention very many dinners and suppers. Tomorrow there is a feast in the Queen's large garden at Trianon . . .We miss none of them.'

Life at Versailles

Following another royal tradition, Louis XVI maintained the vast palace of Versailles, shown in Source 14, as a place to entertain the nobility. Noble families came to live there, in the hope of winning a share of royal government and power. Versailles was also a place where gossip, intrigue and glamorous entertainments flourished freely (see Source 15).

During the reign of Louis XV, Versailles had been a great centre of art, music and theatre, encouraged by the King's mistress, Madame de Pompadour. This had won respect for French culture throughout Europe. But now, under Louis XVI, the elegant, GALANTE world pictured in Source 16 was fading away. Louis XVI's queen, Marie Antoinette (see Source 17) was more interested in escaping from the stuffiness of court life, and in light-hearted amusements. In itself, this was harmless, but in political terms it did not give a very good impression of the monarchy. If the Queen and her friends did not take the royal court seriously, who would?

SOURCE 17

Portrait of Queen Marie Antoinette, painted in 1783 by Louise-Elisabeth Vigée-Lebrun (1755–1842).

1 What ideas do you think passed through Louis XVI's mind while his portrait (Source 11) was being painted?

2 What impression of the personality of Louis XVI do you get from these pages?

3 Do you think Louis XVI was an effective king, able to rule the country well and deal with any crisis?

New ideas

The eighteenth century was an exciting time in which to live if you were a writer, a scientist, or anyone interested in new ideas. In England, Isaac Newton was putting forward revolutionary theories about how the universe was made. The philosopher John Locke was suggesting a totally new way of studying human behaviour. In America, Benjamin Franklin was performing daring experiments with electricity. In Russia, Peter the Great had founded an Academy, where brilliant mathematicians could teach.

In France, in 1751, Denis Diderot (Source 18) and Jean d'Alembert began to publish an encyclopedia (Source 19). They aimed to explain all the recent new discoveries in science and technology to the general public, and they succeeded very well. New ideas were also popularised by books such as Buffon's *Natural History*, a scientific listing of animals (see Source 20), and in many French journals.

Scientific criticism

Diderot and d'Alembert were unlike other scientific publishers. They chose to comment on current events and political ideas, as well as on scientific happenings. They even criticised the French King's claim to rule by Divine Right, and many 'unscientific' beliefs taught by the Church.

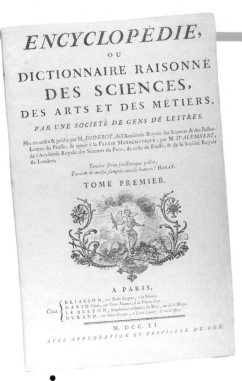

SOURCE 19
Page from the *Encyclopedia* published by Diderot and d'Alembert, 1751–1786.

SOURCE 20
A spread from Buffon's *Natural History*.

SOURCE 18
Denis Diderot (1713–1784)

attainment target 1

1 How do you think each of these groups felt about the American revolution: King Louis and his family; peasants; nobles; bourgeois and priests?

2 Explain why each of these people or groups felt this way.

3 Do you think everyone in the groups above felt the same? Explain your answer.

SOURCE 21
The Caveau (Cellar) Café in Paris. People came here to discuss new ideas and to read.

'Humanity . . . freed from its chains, released from the power of fate and from that of the enemies of progress, advancing with a firm and sure step along the path of truth, virtue and happiness.'

SOURCE 22
A remark made by the philosopher Jean-Jacques Rousseau (1712–1778) describing what he wanted France to be like in future.

Censorship

Diderot and d'Alembert were brave to publish, as the French government punished writers of books they felt were 'damaging to the state'. One leading French scientific thinker, known as Voltaire, was put in prison for composing humorous verses about the royal family which were also very rude. In fact, Voltaire supported royal power but he thought that Louis XVI was not very good at running the government.

The King put people in prison for their writing, but he could not stop people talking. Writers, philosophers and scientists met regularly in cafés (see Source 21) and reading rooms. A new and lively political community was being formed.

Revolution and reform

What sort of ideas did these men discuss? The works of Voltaire were popular, along with the writings of Jean-Jacques Rousseau (see Source 22). After 1775, news of the American Revolution was eagerly waited for. France took America's side in the war against Britain (see Source 23), and many French thinkers were inspired by American ideas. This made some French people look critically at their own society. Perhaps that could also be improved?

However, most people feared change, as Source 24 suggests. They agreed with Montesquieu when he argued that the ideal society should aim at 'a balance of powers'. No single group – royalty, nobles, clergy or bourgeoisie – should be more powerful than the rest. This way of looking at things called for peaceful reform, not violent revolution.

SOURCE 23
Signing the American Declaration of Independence, 1776. This picture was painted in 1819.

SOURCE 24
Comment by an influential French nobleman and philosopher, Charles, Baron de Montesquieu (1689–1755).

'Is it always better to change things than to go on suffering?'

Economic problems

During the 18th century, France was one of the wealthiest and most powerful nations in Europe, largely because of overseas trade (see Source 25). French merchants – wealthy bourgeois and many nobles – invested in plantations in French colonies overseas. The slaves who worked on these plantations were often treated badly, but the merchants did not care. They made high profits by importing valuable tropical goods, especially sugar, cotton, coffee, chocolate, vanilla and spices.

French sea ports on the Atlantic coast, like Dieppe and Le Havre, were rebuilt to cope with the increasing imports. They also profited from the large numbers of slaves brought from Africa to be shipped across the Atlantic.

Elegance and good taste

French industry, though not as profitable or as strong as Britain's, was also a source of wealth. Factories (like the one shown in Source 26) produced high-quality goods, especially silk and cotton textiles, wallpapers, furniture and porcelain (see Source 27). All these went to furnish the homes of the bourgeoisie and nobles. Styles of design and painting popular in France at this time became famous for their elegance and 'good taste' in other countries too.

Trade was one way of moving up the social scale. Rich merchants bought country estates in order to acquire a noble's legal privileges.

Financial crisis

In spite of this flourishing trade, the French royal government had no money. Source 28 shows Louis XVI and Jacques Necker, his chief finance minister, gazing in dismay at empty 'treasure chests'. What had gone wrong? Why, when so many people in the country were obviously prosperous, was the government almost bankrupt?

War

There were two main reasons for this economic crisis. The short-term reason was war. As we saw on page 13, France supported the rebels against Britain during the American Revolution of 1775 to 1783. The government had to borrow vast sums of money to pay for the war, and was left with enormous debts. By 1786, the government deficit – the gap between its income and its expenditure – was three times as big as in 1776.

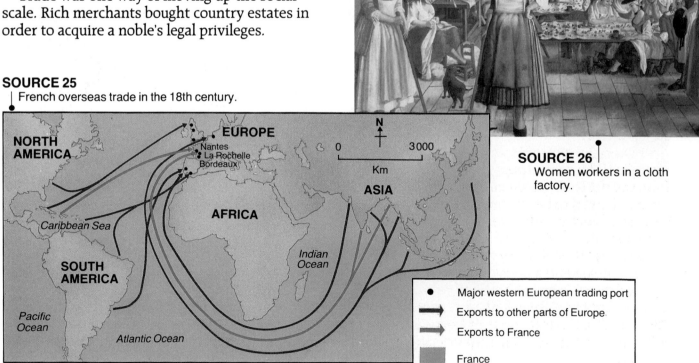

SOURCE 25
French overseas trade in the 18th century.

NORTH AMERICA

EUROPE
Nantes
La Rochelle
Bordeaux

N

0   3000
Km

ASIA

AFRICA

Caribbean Sea

Indian Ocean

SOUTH AMERICA

Pacific Ocean

Atlantic Ocean

•   Major western European trading port
→   Exports to other parts of Europe.
→   Exports to France
▨   France

SOURCE 26
Women workers in a cloth factory.

Elegant French porcelain like this cup and saucer made at Sèvres around 1760, was prized throughout Europe. They are decorated with pure gold.

SOURCE 28
Cartoon showing King Louis XVI (right) and Necker (left) drawn by the British artist, George Cruickshank, in 1788.

---

1 The French economy was based on producing high-priced luxury goods for the rich. What were the economic dangers in this?

2 Why was it so difficult for the King and his ministers to change the unfair system of taxes?

Taxation

The long-term reason for the government's lack of money was its inefficient system of taxation. The task of collecting taxes was 'sold' to officials, known as 'tax-farmers'. These people were paid out of the taxes they collected, and they often kept some back for themselves. This meant that only part of the money paid as taxes ever reached the royal treasury; the rest was 'lost' along the way.

The taxation system was also unfair. Taxes were demanded from poor peasants, but not from the nobles or bourgeoisie. These two groups claimed to be exempt (free) from taxes, because of ancient privileges.

As a result, the King and his ministers faced the hopeless task of trying to raise taxes from people who had no money (see Source 29), while the wealthiest sections of society, who paid nothing, criticised them for bad management. As Calonne, chief finance minister from 1783 to 1787, declared, it was time the system changed (see Source 30).

'Workmen today need twice as much money to keep them alive, yet they earn no more than fifty years ago'.

SOURCE 29
Comment by parish priest in Normandy, northern France, in the 1780s.

It is impossible to tax further, ruinous to keep on borrowing, and not enough to confine ourselves to economical reforms . . . the only means of managing finally to put the finances truly in order, must consist in revitalising the entire state by re-moulding all that is evil in its workings.

SOURCE 30
Remark by Charles-Alexandre de Calonne, Louis XVI's chief finance minister, in 1787.

Government in crisis

For many years, there had been tensions when *parlements* – especially in Paris – refused to accept new royal laws. The *parlements* had a right to do this if they disagreed with royal policies. To King Louis, it seemed as if *parlements* acted to protect their own interests, not for the good of society. In particular, they blocked attempts at reforming the system by which taxes were collected.

In 1787, Louis and his ministers summoned an assembly of *Notables* (important people) to help them solve France's economic crisis. The *Notables* met and discussed, but would not agree to the government's plans for tax reforms. Meanwhile, the economic problems grew worse. There were demonstrations in provincial cities, supporting local *parlements* against the King. In Paris, starving citizens accused the government of a 'famine plot' – a plan to starve them into obedience – and rioted. In desperation, royal ministers agreed to the *parlements'* calls for a meeting of the Estates-General – the ancient ruling council of France.

Voting rights

Before this meeting could take place, there were more disagreements. Who should attend the Estates-General? Traditionally, it was made up of deputies (elected representatives) from three different groups: First Estate (clergy), Second Estate (nobles), and Third Estate (everyone else). The last time it met, in 1614, there had been an equal number of deputies for each group. Each estate had also voted separately.

- town-dwellers want the same rights and privileges as nobles.
- peasants want freedom from feudal taxes.
- peasants want fewer and fairer royal taxes.
- tithes should be used to support the ordinary parish clergy who helped villagers, and not paid to noble clergy who used it to support their extravagant lifestyle.
- the countryside should not be exploited to make town-dwellers – including nobles – richer.

SOURCE 31

Demands made in the *cahiers* (notebooks listing grievances) drawn up by the ordinary Frenchmen who elected the deputies to represent the Third Estate at the 1789 Estates-General.

SOURCE 32

The meeting of the Estates-General, 5 May 1789.

SOURCE 33
The historic meeting at the indoor tennis court, June 1789, attended by a few nobles, a few members of the clergy and the Third Estate.

'Go and tell those who have sent you that we sit here by the will of the people, and that we shall not leave except by force of bayonets.'

SOURCE 34
Spoken by the Comte de Mirabeau, on behalf of the Third Estate, while they were meeting at the indoor tennis court, in 1789.

Demands of the Third Estate

The Third Estate now demanded double the number of deputies because they claimed that their members were playing a larger part in French life. They also wanted all sections of the Estates-General to meet at the same time. In this way, the Third Estate would be able to out-vote the other two, who they expected to side with the King.

Third Estate deputies were not poor or disadvantaged like the majority of French people. They were lawyers, officials and rich bourgeois. But, encouraged by other politicians, they felt they were the true 'voice of the nation'. They knew that ordinary people had many grievances which needed to be put right (See Source 31).

'Thus it was that in France the judiciary, the clergy, the rich, gave their original impulse to the Revolution. The people appeared on the scene only later.'

SOURCE 35
Comment by the revolutionary leader, Robespierre, looking back at what happened in 1789.

The start of a Revolution?

The Third Estate's demands had still not been satisfied when the Estates-General held its first meeting in May 1789 (see Source 32). It seemed unlikely that the King and his ministers would give in. The Third Estate was angry and continued to demand that the 'voice of the nation' be heard. On 17 June, they re-named themselves the 'National Assembly'.

Three days later their meeting hall was locked, on government orders. This was, in fact, accidental, but they felt it was a royal attack on their rights and they were furious. They rushed to find another room, and decided to occupy an indoor tennis court (see Source 33). There, they took an oath to stay put until their demands had been met. By 25 June, they had been joined by a majority of deputies from the clergy, plus influential nobles like Mirabeau (see Source 34). On 27 June, the King gave in, and ordered all three Estates to meet together. Was this the start of a Revolution? As Source 35 suggests, the answer is 'yes'.

> **attainment target 2**
>
> 'The French Revolution was begun by good men on good principles' – Tom Paine, writing a few years later.
>
> 1 Is this a statement of fact or an opinion? Explain your answer.
>
> 2 Do you agree with this interpretation? Explain your answer.
>
> 3 How far do the sources in these pages support this interpretation?
>
> 4 Tom Paine was a supporter of the Revolution. How does that affect your judgement of his interpretation?

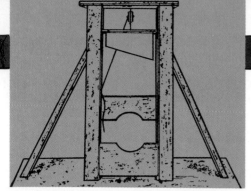

The Revolution

AIMS

In this Unit we will look at the events of the French Revolution, during the years 1789 to 1799. We will consider why the Revolution began when it did, and what it hoped to achieve. We will look at the personalities involved, from the royal family to the rebel leaders. Finally, we will see how people reacted to the Revolution, both in France and overseas.

The Revolution begins

On 20 June, 1789, the date of the Tennis Court Oath, the situation was tense, but not dangerous. The King, his officials and his army were still in control of France. At Versailles, nobles, priests and deputies from the Third Estate attending the meeting of the Estates-General, were protesting against the King, but they were not at war with him.

Yet within weeks, angry mobs in Paris could be heard chanting songs like the one in Source 1 and there were riots, murders and massacres (see Source 2). In the countryside, peasants drew up *cahiers*, or lists of complaints against the government, and attacked nobles' property. The French Revolution had begun.

SOURCE 1
Popular song, heard on the streets of Paris, 1789.

'It will be, it will be, it will be
We'll hang noblemen from the street-lights . . .
Freedom will be ours for ever
We'll put an end to cruel tyrants . . .'

Events of the Revolution

1789 (14 July)
Bastille attacked; the Revolution begins.

1789 (July-August)
Grand Peur in the countryside – attacks on nobles' property.

1789 (August)
Declaration of the Rights of Man and the Citizen.

1789 (October)
Mob marches to Versailles and captures royal family.

1789 (November)
State take-over of Church property; National Assembly now runs France.

1791 (June)
Royal family tries to escape.

1792 (August)
Fear of invasion after France declares war on Austria; massacres in Paris.

1792 (September)
French troops defeat invaders at Valmy; France attacks nearby lands.

1792 (September)
Monarchy abolished.

1792 (December)
Louis XVI on trial.

1793 (January)
Louis XVI executed.

1793 (March)
France now at war with most other European powers.

1793 (March)
Vendée revolt by anti-revolutionaries.

1793 (April)
Committee of Public Safety (radicals) now controls government.

1793 (May)
Anti-revolutionary revolts in Lyon and Paris. Disputes among revolutionary leaders.

1793 (June)
Girondin (moderate) leaders arrested; reign of Terror begins.

1793 (July)
Marat assassinated; Jacobin (radical) leader Robespierre siezes power.

1793 (August)
Conscription introduced.

1793 (October)
Marie Antoinette executed, also many Girondins (moderates).

1794 (October)
New revolutionary religion introduced.

1794 (April)
Danton (radical) executed.

1794 (July)
Robespierre executed; Terror ends.

1795 (November)
Directory (moderates) now rules France; wars continue in Europe.

1799 (November)
Napoleon seizes power.

SOURCE 2
The march to Versailles, October 1789. Officers of the Royal Guard who resisted the revolutionaries were beheaded and their heads carried on spikes.

Reasons for the Revolution

Why did the Revolution break out in 1789? There were many different reasons. Some were long-term, others were more immediate.

In the countryside:
People were discontented, because of:
- poverty among the peasants
- wide gap between rich and poor
- heavy taxes
- privileges of the nobles

New developments in the 18th century:
- growing wealth of the bourgeoisie
- low wages for town workers
- new scientific and philosophical ideas
- the Revolution in America

Personalities:
- Louis XVI was lazy and incompetent
- Marie Antoinette was extravagant
- their son was dying, so they neglected politics
- people did not trust royal ministers
- new leaders emerged in the Estates-General

Events, 1787 to 1789:
- the government ran short of money
- calling the Estates-General made people hope for change
- harvests were bad and people were hungry

What were the aims of the Revolution?

There is no simple answer. Protesters wanted to get rid of a system which they felt was unfair. They hoped the Estates-General would find a solution. As Sources 3, 4, 5 and 6 reveal, people reacted to the Revolution in different ways.

'I believe that some extraordinary event is likely to occur'.

SOURCE 3
Comment by Antoine-Joseph Barnarve (1761–1793), a lawyer who supported the Revolution in its early days.

'Bliss was it in that dawn to be alive. And to be young, was very heaven.'

SOURCE 4
From 'The Prelude', a poem by the English poet, William Wordsworth, who visited France in 1789.

Like everyone else, I was shaking with terror . . . waiting for the royalists to come and murder us . . . (but) we went about our business as we would on any other day.

SOURCE 5
Revolutionary violence in 1792 remembered by Marie-Victoire Monnard, an apprentice seamstress, aged 13.

'My ambition is that one day I may live, in the country, with a wife and children, with books for my spare time, and, for the rest, time to spare for the poor among my neighbours.'

SOURCE 6
Louis-Antoine de Saint-Just (1767–1794), a young revolutionary, explaining what he hoped for after the Revolution.

The events of 1789

Today, over 200 years after the French Revolution, 14 July is a national holiday in France. Why is this date so important? It is because, on that day in 1789, a crowd of angry people in Paris rushed to the royal prison called the Bastille, forced their way in and released the prisoners. They murdered the governor and many guards (see Source 7). 'Bastille Day' marks the start of the French Revolution.

There were, in fact, only 7 prisoners inside the Bastille, and none had been imprisoned for political reasons. To the Paris mob, however, the Bastille was important as a symbol of royal power. They hated the King and his ministers, and wanted to run the country for themselves.

SOURCE 7
The attack on the Bastille, 14 July 1789. A painting made soon after the event, by Dubois.

'The aristocracy is at an end, the clergy wobbles on the edge of mindlessness, and the third Estate doesn't really understand what is going on. Only the victorious mob is happy, with nothing to lose, all to gain.'

SOURCE 8
Comment by Count Axel von Fersen, a close friend of the royal family, 1789.

Mob rule?

Onlookers, like the ROYALIST sympathiser quoted in Source 8, realised that the attack on the Bastille marked a new kind of discontent in France. For the first time, ordinary people were taking part in politics. Representatives from all sections of French society – nobles, clergy, bourgeoisie and ordinary citizens – were united against the King. For a while, it even seemed as if ordinary people were the revolutionary leaders. As well as massacres in Paris, there were murders in the countryside. Documents recording peasants' duty to pay tax, and nobles' ancient privileges, were destroyed by villagers. There were riots in many towns, too. People called this hot, dangerous, summertime the Great Fear (see Source 9).

> **attainment target 1**

1 List three long-term and three short-term causes of the French Revolution. Explain how you have decided which are long- and which are short-term.

2 Choose one example of each and explain how it led to revolution.

3 Describe how money and finance link several of the causes listed on page 19.

4 Which of the causes listed do you think was the most important? Explain your answer.

SOURCE 9
Transporting corpses after fighting between royalists and revolutionaries.

Parisian women march to Versailles, October 1789.

We want bread!

In Paris, rioting continued throughout the autumn. It came to a climax on 5 and 6 October, when thousands of women, exasperated at not being able to buy food for their families, marched to the royal palace at Versailles (see Source 10). They surrounded the King, and forced him and his family to come back to Paris with them. Even though the royal family lodged in another royal palace, the Tuileries, from now on the King was in their power.

The Rights of Man

Members of the National Assembly disagreed about whether the summer's violence – some of which was directed against their own property – was acceptable. Most thought it was not, but they had to show support for the mob's revolutionary enthusiasm, to protect their homes and businesses from further damage. Of course, many Assembly members also genuinely believed that the time had come to make changes to the way France was run. So, on 4 August, they passed a decree abolishing FEUDALISM, the ancient network of rights, privileges and taxes which the peasants hated so much. They followed this, on 26 August, by the solemn 'Declaration of the Rights of Man and the Citizen' (Source 11). This set out clearly what the Assembly hoped the Revolution would achieve. You can read more about it on page 22.

SOURCE 11
A revolutionary painting recording the Declaration of the Rights of Man and the Citizen.

Revolutionary reforms

Late in 1789, two new questions concerned the National Assembly. How could they stop the Revolution leading to complete ANARCHY (lack of government), and what new laws should they make to replace the old ones? Forceful speakers appeared, arguing for dozens of different policies. As one of the Assembly's leaders, Mirabeau, (pictured in Source 12), complained, it was not always easy to keep eager revolutionaries under control (Source 13).

Freedom and equality

As we saw on page 21, the National Assembly had approved a 'Declaration of the Rights of Man and the Citizen'. It stated bravely that:

- Men are born and remain free.
- They have equal rights to liberty, property, security and freedom from tyranny.
- Laws should reflect citizens' wishes.
- All citizens should be able to make their political views known.
- Liberty is the freedom to do anything that doesn't harm anybody else.
- Everyone should have the right of free speech.

SOURCE 12
The Comte de Mirabeau (1749–1791), painted in 1790.

'When you agree to take charge of a revolution, the difficulty is not making it move, but controlling it.'

SOURCE 13
Comment by Mirabeau, looking back on the events of the Revolution shortly before his death in 1791.

SOURCE 14
The Cordeliers Church, in Paris, being destroyed following the State take-over of Church property.

Active citizens

How could this Declaration be put into practice? Partly by giving the Assembly more power. In 1789, the deputies changed Louis XVI's title from 'King of France' to 'King of the French'. Now the land no longer belonged to him. In 1791, they passed laws to allow more people to take part in politics. The richest men (65 per cent of them) were called 'active citizens'. They could vote, and choose judges, bishops, tax collectors and members of the Assembly. Poorer people and women could not vote.

The legal and local government systems were also reformed. Inherited noble titles were abolished; everyone was now equal in the eyes of the law. Trial by jury was introduced, and torture was banned. Instead of the old regions, ruled over by *parlements*, 83 new *départements* were created, controlled by central government.

ACTIVITY

Work in a small group to discuss these questions:
1 If you were drawing up a list of new laws to improve 18th century French society, what would be the three most important reforms?
2 Do you think the people who drew up the Declaration of the Rights of Man and the Citizen did a good job?
3 What three new laws would you like to introduce to improve our society today?

SOURCE 15
Assignats being exchanged for cash by country people.

A national Church?

In November 1789, the Assembly decided to 'nationalise' the church. It distrusted priests' vows of obedience to the Pope in Rome, and disliked the Church's support for the King. Church lands and buildings were taken over and destroyed (see Source 14) or sold off, using *assignats* (paper money). You can see these in Source 15. Monasteries and nunneries were closed down, and priests were asked to swear loyalty to the state. Many refused.

Celebrations

Not everyone in France benefited from these changes, and not everyone agreed with them, but it was becoming dangerous to speak out. Defiant priests and old-style royalists were put in prison. Most French people, especially those in Paris, probably shared the views of the speaker quoted in Source 16. They happily joined in celebrations, like the festival shown in Source 17, to mark the Revolution's first 'anniversary' on 14 July 1790.

'A new political structure is being built. I do not say it is absolutely perfect, but it is sufficient to guarantee liberty.'

SOURCE 16
Remark by the Marquis de Lafayette (1757–1834), a nobleman who sympathised with the Revolution.

SOURCE 17
Celebrations known as 'The Festival of the Federation', held in Paris on 14 July 1790.

SOURCE 18
Popular woodcut showing the royal family making their bid to escape from France, 1791.

Kill the king

For over a year, the King and his family lived like prisoners in Paris. Observers reported that Louis seemed depressed and Marie Antoinette looked old and ill. Many of their friends fled abroad for safety. The King and Queen sent secret letters to them, and to royalists in France. They also asked foreign rulers for help, especially Marie Antoinette's family in Austria.

'If this country ceases to be a monarchy it will be entirely the fault of Louis XVI. Blunder upon blunder . . . have been the destruction of his reign.'

Lord Gower, a British aristocrat

'The absence of a king is more desirable than his presence . . . He has abdicated (given up) his throne by having fled from his post.'

Tom Paine, a British campaigner for freedom

'We will eat her heart and liver.'

The mob of French citizens

SOURCE 19
Comments by people from different levels of society with different views about the King and Queen.

Escape to Varennes

On 20 June 1791, the royal family decided to try to escape. At night, (with Louis disguised as a servant) they left Paris in a horse-drawn coach (Source 18). They headed towards Luxembourg, where the Emperor of Austria had 8,000 troops. There were also loyal French soldiers nearby. But the King was stopped at Varennes, a village not far from the border. The local postmaster recognised him from his portrait on a 50-*livre* (pound) note. Louis refused to run away, because that would mean leaving his wife and children behind. The royal family were sent back to Paris under armed guard. Hostile crowds shouted insults all along the way.

'Louis the False'

What did Louis think about the Revolution? In public, he claimed to support the various revolutionary governments, and to accept their new laws. However he left a note behind him when he tried to escape, protesting that he felt injured and powerless, and that the Revolution was ruining France. After that, very few people trusted him. He became known as 'Louis the False'. Source 19 gives three comments made about Louis and Marie Antoinette after their bid to escape.

The end of royal power

In August 1792, crowds attacked the Tuileries (Source 20). Over 700 soldiers were hacked to death, and the King and Queen were threatened. It was a terrifying moment. From now on, the King and all royalists were treated like traitors. They were put in prison, and the King was deprived of all his powers.

The following month (September), Prussian and Austrian troops marched towards Paris, hoping to free the King. Frightened of what might happen if they reached the city, panic-stricken crowds attacked the prisons and killed the royalists there.

Once again, Louis' life was spared by the mob. But for how long? On 21 September, in the new Assembly (now called the Convention), members voted to abolish the monarchy, and set up a republic. The King was no longer part of government. To many people, he seemed a dangerous, useless burden to France.

Innocent or guilty?

In December 1792, King Louis was put on trial. The Convention accused him of over 30 'crimes against the state'. Sources 21 and 22 record what two leading deputies from the Convention said in court. All 693 deputies found Louis guilty, and the majority (374) voted for his death. He was executed by guillotine (Source 23) on 21 January 1793. On the scaffold, he said, 'I die innocent'.

attainment target 1

Look at the following reasons for Louis' execution:

a) His policy as King up to 1789;   b) his attitude to the Revolution;   c) the flight to Varennes;   d) foreign troops invading France;   e) the declaration of a republic.

1 Choose two of these reasons and say how they helped bring about Louis' execution.

2 Which of the reasons above were his fault and which were not?

3 Which do you think was the most important reason? Compare your choice with those you rejected.

'Monarchy is not a crime – it is THE crime.'

SOURCE 22
Comment by Louis-Antoine Saint-Just (1767–1794), a young revolutionary leader.

SOURCE 23
Souvenir plate showing the execution of Louis XVI.

SOURCE 20
Parisian citizens attack the royal palace of the Tuileries, 10 August 1792.

'You should fill tyrants with terror – I vote for the penalty of death..'

SOURCE 21
Spoken by Georges-Jacques Danton (1759–1794), one of the revolutionary leaders, at Louis XVI's trial.

Reactions at home

The execution of the King in January 1793 changed France for ever. Some people thought this was a good thing; some did not. For royalists, it marked the end of 'the good old days' and the beginning of a nightmare period of uncertainty and chaos. For revolutionaries, it was the start of a bright new future for republican France.

Even among those who sympathised with the Revolution, there were disagreements. Deputies elected to the Confederation – the new government of France – were mostly MODERATES. They supported firm law and order, and wanted to protect private property. More and more, they found themselves quarrelling with leaders of the ordinary people of Paris – the 'sans-culottes'.

SOURCE 25
A meeting of the Patriotic (revolutionary) Women's Club in Paris.

'The moment has arrived for women to throw away their shameful laziness . . . Ignorance, pride and men's power have kept them quiet for too long. Let us return to the past when our proud fore-mothers spoke at public meetings and fought with weapons alongside the men.'

SOURCE 26
Part of a speech by Théroigne de Méricourt, one of the leading women revolutionaries.

SOURCE 24
A popular Parisian singer, Chenard, who supported the sans-culottes, in typical sans-culotte clothes.

Equality

'Sans-culottes' meant 'no breeches', or 'wearing rough, working clothes' (see Source 24). Noblemen often wore waistcoats and knee-breeches made of embroidered satin, while sans-culottes wore plain shirts, long baggy trousers and woollen jackets. They often chose the revolutionary colours of red, white and blue. Even sans-culottes who could afford better clothes preferred this 'uniform'; it was a way of showing that they believed all men were equal.

Disagreements

Sans-culottes clashed with the deputies over three main issues. They wanted all adult men to be given the right to vote. They demanded regular food supplies and low prices. Most RADICAL of all, they wanted the amount of land, money or property that anyone could own to be limited by law, so that wealth could be shared out equally.

Revolutionary women

Ordinary women played an important part in revolutionary events but, on the whole, their contribution was ignored by the (male) deputies, and by the (male) leaders of the *sans-culottes*. The 'Declaration of the Rights of Man and the Citizen' did not include women in its reforms. In the early years of the Revolution, women's groups (like the one in Source 25) met to discuss politics. Some carried weapons, but they were quickly banned. This did not stop leaders like Théroigne de Méricourt (quoted in Source 26) urging women to fight for their beliefs alongside revolutionary men.

Provincial rebels

There had always been differences of opinion between go-ahead Paris, and the slower, more cautious, country districts of France. Now, in 1793, these quarrels turned into a bloody war. Many people living in the PROVINCES felt that the Parisian *sans-culottes* were too radical. They thought that the nationalisation of the Church and the execution of the King had been wrong. Source 27 shows the areas where these views had most support. Thousands of men and women were killed (see Source 28). Source 29 shows fighting close to the city of Lyon. Peasants and town-dwellers attacked revolutionary leaders and other republicans.

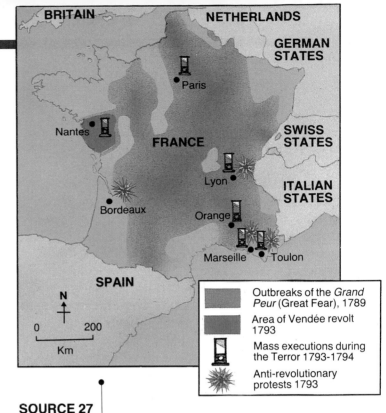

SOURCE 27
Royalist and revolutionary areas of France.

'Every wickedness you can imagine. About 50 people were beaten and their heads shaved. It seems that the women were most unpopular with the attackers. Three died a little later. The remainder are still weak.'

SOURCE 28
Description of fighting between revolutionaries and royalists near Rouen, in northern France, 1792.

1 Read about the demands made by the *sans-culottes* on page 26. How can you tell from these that the *sans-culottes* were city-based?

2 Why do you think there was more support for the Revolution in the city of Paris than in the countryside?

3 Why are clothes so often a sign of rebellion? Give some present day examples of this.

SOURCE 29
Fighting between revolutionaries and royalists in the important city of Lyon, in southern France, 1795.

Reactions abroad

On page 25 we saw that, in 1792, Parisian citizens had been frightened when enemy troops began to advance, so they killed royalist prisoners. In fact, the citizens' fears were unnecessary. The threatened invasion never came. Revolutionary troops attacked the enemy armies at Valmy, on the road to Paris, and they retreated in confusion. The invaders had not expected these 'rebel' soldiers to be so strong.

Exporting the Revolution

This surprising victory gave great encouragement to the revolutionary leaders. It made them think it might be possible for France to 'export' its revolutionary ideas. Source 30 tells us what two revolutionaries hoped to achieve. By the end of 1792, French soldiers were advancing into Belgium, Germany and Savoy, as you can see from Source 31.

France's revolutionary ambitions horrified most governments in Europe. In 1793, England, Spain and the Netherlands joined Austria and Prussia, which were already enemies of France. Austria, led by its confident new Emperor Francis II (see Source 32), was especially eager to attack. Austrians were outraged when Marie Antoinette was guillotined in October 1793.

In 1794, France conquered the Netherlands, and set up a revolutionary government there. A stirring new song, called 'La Marseillaise', was composed for these revolutionary soldiers to sing. In 1795, it was adopted as the French national anthem, and it remains so today. You can see the words and music in Source 33.

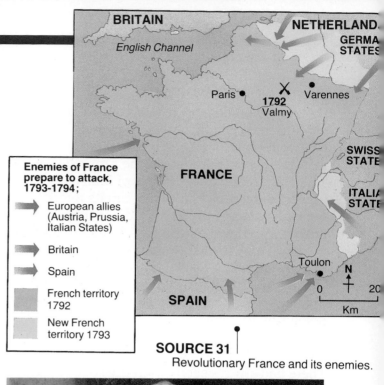

SOURCE 31
Revolutionary France and its enemies.

Map legend:
Enemies of France prepare to attack, 1793-1794:
- European allies (Austria, Prussia, Italian States)
- Britain
- Spain
- French territory 1792
- New French territory 1793

SOURCE 32
Emperor Francis II of Austria (1768–1835), a determined opponent of revolutionary France.

Renewing the state

Revolutionary leaders in France thought that war should be encouraged for another reason, too – it was good for people at home. It allowed them to forget their quarrels with one another while they were united against a foreign enemy. As Source 34 reveals, it could also be used by the government to send critics of the Revolution out of the country.

A war of ideas

European nations did not fight France only on the battlefield. They took part in a war of ideas. The Irishman, Edmund Burke, wrote 'Reflections on the Revolution in France' (1790), which fiercely criticised revolutionary leaders. English artists portrayed the French as bloodthirsty monsters in cartoons such as Source 35.

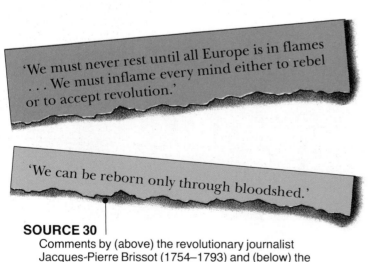

'We must never rest until all Europe is in flames ... We must inflame every mind either to rebel or to accept revolution.'

'We can be reborn only through bloodshed.'

SOURCE 30
Comments by (above) the revolutionary journalist Jacques-Pierre Brissot (1754–1793) and (below) the revolutionary political hostess Manon Roland (1754–1793).

SOURCE 33
Song-sheet showing the French Army of the Rhine, marching to fight in Germany, plus words and music of the Marseillaise.

SOURCE 35
Cartoon by the English artist, James Gillray, after Louis XVI's bid to escape from France. Gillray has drawn the members of the National Assembly as monsters, gleefully discussing what to do with the King.

 France . . . needs war to consolidate its freedom. It needs war to get rid of the wickedness of tyranny. It needs war to drive out those who might poison liberty.

SOURCE 34
Another piece of revolutionary propaganda written by Brissot (see Source 30).

Ending slavery

There were few slaves in France itself, but the economy of most French colonies, particularly in the Caribbean, depended on slave labour. During the Revolution, many politicians argued that it was wrong to fight for equality at home, while ignoring the lack of freedom in French lands overseas. In 1788, they had founded 'Friends of Black People', a campaigning group which aimed to abolish slavery. Slaves in the French colony of San Domingo (Haiti) rebelled in 1794, encouraged by revolutionary events in France. Their courageous leader, Toussaint L'Ouverture, is pictured in Source 36.

SOURCE 36
Toussaint L'Ouverture (left, front of picture) and his troops in Haiti.

Revolutionary leaders

All revolutions need someone to lead them, to make new policies and to decide what action is required to carry them out. We have seen how, in the early days of the Revolution, two very different groups were active: deputies of the National Assembly (and the later assemblies that followed it) and the Paris mob, known as the *sans-culottes*.

Individual revolutionaries

Individuals also acted as leaders, like the churchman, Canon Sieyès of Chartres, who drafted important schemes for reform. More practical leaders included two nobles: the Marquis de Lafayette and the Comte de Mirabeau. Lafayette had fought for the rebels during the American Revolution. He commanded the French army until 1792, when he left France, shocked by the King's execution. Mirabeau (page 22) was a rousing speaker, who played a leading part in the events of summer 1789. However he thought the *sans-culottes* were too extreme, and secretly supported the King. If he had not died in 1791, he would probably have been executed as a traitor.

There were other revolutionary leaders who were not nobles. They met in cafés and SALONS of Paris to discuss their ideas. *Salons* were rooms in private houses, where people who shared similar ideas met. Privacy was needed because rival groups soon began to hold different views.

Girondins and Jacobins

The two most important FACTIONS were the GIRONDINS and the JACOBINS. At first, they had been allies. However, moderate Girondins, like Brissot (Source 37) and Madame Roland (see Source 38) criticised Jacobins' radical ideas. Later, many Girondins were executed by the Jacobins, led by Danton (Source 39) and Robespierre (Source 40).

SOURCE 37
Jacques-Pierre Brissot (1754–1793) Journalist and campaigner. Founder of anti-slavery society: Friends of Black People (see page 29). Member of Legislative Assembly; thought Paris mob was too violent. Executed by Jacobins October 1793.

'At fourteen, as now, I was about five feet tall, having reached full growth. I had trim legs, very well-shaped feet . . . straight shoulders, a steady and graceful posture, and brisk, light footsteps. My face was not really remarkable, save for its genuine freshness and much sweetness. My mouth is rather large; you could notice a thousand people who are prettier but no child with a more tender and seductive smile . . . My complexion is striking . . . my skin soft, my arms rounded, my hands not small, but attractive with long slender fingers suggesting cleverness combined with grace . . .'

SOURCE 38
Manon Roland (1754–1793) From a Paris craft-worker's family. Clever and ambitious. Held a salon where the Girondins met. With her husband, very active in politics. Arrested by Jacobins and executed November 1793.

> attainment target 3

1 What do Sources 41 and 42 tell us about Charlotte Corday?

2 Which of Sources 42 and 43 is more valuable for finding out about her motives?

3 What problems of reliability does Source 43 present?

4 What can we use Source 43 to tell us about in spite of its unreliability?

SOURCE 40
Maximilien Robespierre (1758–1794) Educated as a lawyer. Member of Legislative Assembly and a Jacobin. Called 'the incorruptible', because he did not make money out of his position. Wanted to exterminate 'enemies of the Revolution' (see page 32). Executed by new, moderate leaders appalled by his violence, July 1794.

'Oh my native land – your misfortunes are breaking my heart; all I can sacrifice to you is my life.'

SOURCE 41
From a note found pinned to Charlotte Corday's clothes, after her execution.

SOURCE 39
Georges Danton (1759–1794) Educated as a lawyer. Rich, popular, very powerful politician. Originally supported the Jacobins, but disagreed with their policy of mass execution (see page 32). Executed on Robespierre's orders April 1794.

The Murder of Marat

One of the best-known events of the Revolution happened in 1793, when the Girondin supporter, Charlotte Corday, killed Jean-Paul Marat, a popular Jacobin, in his bath. Source 41 reports Corday's words explaining why she committed the murder. Source 42 shows the murder scene. Source 43 comes from the revolutionary Tribunal (court) proceedings, organised by the Jacobins. Corday was tried by this court, and executed the same day.

SOURCE 42
A contemporary painting of the murder of Marat by Charlotte Corday.

Jean-Paul Marat (1744–1793) Doctor, admired by Parisians. Member of the Assembly. Ran newspaper 'The People's Friend', criticising Girondins and all rich people. Feared by some for his violent policies.

Charlotte Corday (1768–1793) Educated woman, active in politics in Normandy. Supported Girondins. Believed that Marat's policies would lead to terrible bloodshed, so killed him. Hated by Jacobins. Executed July 1793.

'She was a woman who gave up womanliness . . . romantic love and other tendernesses no longer affect a woman who seeks knowledge, wit, scholarship, philosophy, and who hopes for personal fame. Decent men dislike such females . . .'

SOURCE 43
From the record kept by the Revolutionary Tribunal, 1793.

SOURCE 44

Cartoon criticising Robespierre. He is shown executing himself, surrounded by guillotines and tombstones.

The Terror

From March 1793 and August 1794, between 14,000 and 17,000 French men and women were executed. A further 24,000 died in prison, or were killed by revolutionary armies. A 'modern' French machine, the guillotine (Source 44), was used for executions. It was invented as a kinder way of killing people than the axe, but it soon became feared as a symbol of revolutionary power. Looking back, people called the years 1793–1794 'the Terror'. Why did this bloodshed take place?

SOURCE 45

A meeting of a revolutionary tribunal (court) held on 2–3 September, 1792.

Defending the Revolution

In 1793, leaders of the Revolution felt under threat. They faced rebellion from royalists at home and invasion from enemies abroad. To cope with these dangers, a Committee of Public Safety was appointed. Its most important members were Jacobins: Danton and Robespierre. Committee members felt it was their duty to defend the Revolution, at all costs. In this emergency situation, the safest thing would be to rid France of anyone who dared criticise revolutionary ideas.

In June 1793, Girondin members of the Convention were expelled, and a new constitution was introduced. In September 1793, the Committee passed a law saying that all people suspected of anti-revolutionary views should be put in prison. If found guilty, they should be killed. You can see suspects being interrogated in Source 45. Neighbourhood 'thought police' were appointed, and conscription – forced enrolment – to the 'Peoples' Army' was introduced.

'The only way to establish a Republic is to utterly destroy all opposition.'

'I recognise as a patriot only that man who will, if necessary, betray his father, mother and sister, and then drink a glass of their blood on the scaffold.'

SOURCE 46

The views of two Jacobins during the Terror.

Who was killed?			
By rank in society:		By region:	
Nobles	900	Paris	2,600
Lawyers/officials	300	Vendée (area of	
Bourgeoisie	3,500	royalist rebellion)	8,700
Priests	900		
Ordinary workers	4,500	Royalist cities	2,000
Peasants	4,000	Royalist south	1,300
Others	200	Others	2,000
Total	14,300	Total	16,600
(Exact totals are impossible; it depends which sources are used.)			

Reactions to the Terror

Reactions to the Terror were mixed. Even its leaders could not agree whether the policy of mass executions was right. But those who dared voice their opposition (like Danton) were sent to the guillotine. Source 46 shows how some Committee members justified their actions; Source 47 reports a horrified comment from a moderate onlooker.

A new France

Not all the policies introduced by the Committee of Public Safety were violent. Some were designed to help ordinary people, for example fixing maximum prices for food and distributing guilty suspects' goods to the poor. A new calendar (Source 48) was established, to mark the beginning of the revolutionary era. In 1794, slavery was abolished.

A new way of speaking to other people, using the familiar form of the word 'you', ('tu') rather than the formal 'vous', was introduced. Like the modern word 'comrade', it was meant to show that, after the Revolution, everyone was equal. Villages and towns changed their names; for example, Roiville (Kingstown) became Peupleville (Peopletown). Patriotic parents named their children after revolutionary heroes, like Voltaire. Others abandoned 'Christian' names and chose names from nature, such as *Blé* (Wheat), *Myrthe* (Myrtle) or *Safran* (Saffron).

Look at the lists opposite of people killed during the terror.

1 Which group suffered the most deaths?

2 What do these figures tell us about:
- the people most affected by the Revolution?
- the people most hated or feared by Jacobins?
- the differences between Paris and elsewhere?

3 Is it true that the Revolution was a rebellion of poor people against a rich ruling class?

> The Revolution . . . is devouring its own children.

SOURCE 47
Comment made by the Frenchman, Pierre-Victurnien Vernigand during the Terror. Compare this with Source 46.

SOURCE 48
The new calendar introduced to mark the beginning of the revolutionary era.

The Revolutionary Calendar

The Convention made a new calendar for France. It had 12 months, but each month was divided into three weeks of 10 days each. The months were as follows:–

Vendémiaire	Grape harvest	22 September–21 October
Brumaire	Misty	22 October–20 November
Frimaire	Frosty	21 November–20 December
Nivôse	Snowy	21 December–19 January
Pluviose	Rainy	20 January–18 February
Ventôse	Windy	19 February–20 March
Germinal	Month of buds	21 March–19 April
Floréal	Flower month	20 April–19 May
Prairial	Meadow month	20 May–18 June
Messidor	Harvest month	19 June–18 July
Thermidor	Month of heat	19 July–17 August
Fructidor	Month of fruits	18 August–16 September

The five days left over at the end of the year were holidays. Each new year started on 22 September (or 1 Vendémiaire), with 1 Vendémiaire 1793 marking the start of the first year of the Republic.

The end of the Revolution

Robespierre and his allies on the Committee of Public Safety were guillotined in July 1794. The Terror was over. Better still, from the new government's point of view, its terrifying policies were no longer necessary. Moderate politicians had shown that they could win control.

Throughout France, the strongest feeling was probably one of relief. Even if most French people did not agree with British onlookers, who called Robespierre a 'butcher', they felt that too many 'enemies of the Revolution' had died. Even today, historians do not all hold the same opinions about Robespierre's career. Was he simply power-mad, or was he boldly trying to force through policies which he really believed would help the ordinary citizens of France?

'The rebels' guns are aiming at the city . . . the outskirts are packed with squads of citizens bearing pikes and a few old-style muskets . . . the people seem determined not to be disarmed. Women have gathered in every street, and are making uproar . . . '

SOURCE 49
From Paris police records.

SOURCE 50
Rich, fashionable, anti-revolutionary young men, known as *Incroyables* ('Unbelievables').

SOURCE 51
Troops led by Napoleon Bonaparte defeat citizens rebelling against the government, 5 October 1795.

Reconstruction

The politicians who took over from Robespierre had a difficult task. They had to restore calm and trust in the government and rebuild trade and industry, while supporting the Revolution. They also had to control royalist rebels in the provinces. As Source 49 reveals, fighting was still going on. In Paris, Jacobins were attacked by rich, anti-revolutionary young men (see Source 50), and the Jacobin club was closed down. Officials appointed during the Terror lost their jobs and even the word 'revolutionary' was banned. On 5 October 1795, a group of royalists attempted to seize power (see Source 51). They were defeated, thanks to the quick thinking of a young officer named Napoleon.

The Directory

At the end of 1795, five politicians known as 'the Directory' took over the government (see Source 52). Their policies were anti-royalist, and they did not want the Terror to return, but they were not popular (see Source 53). They struggled to cope with France's economic crisis. As always, it had to confront many rival groups with different views, all wanting power.

The Directory felt that the Revolution was only likely to survive if France was united against a foreign enemy. It therefore encouraged wars against other European states. However, in spite of victories, such as Napoleon's success at the battle of Rivoli in 1796 (pictured in Source 54), the new government still did not win peoples' support. By 1799, secret groups of conspirators were seeking change.

SOURCE 52
The first public meeting of the Directory, November 1795. A 19th century engraving.

Royalist or republican?

One group, the royalists, thought it would be a good idea to invite Louis XVI's brother to head a new national government, though with strictly limited powers. The other group, the republicans, hated the idea of a return to royal rule. They wanted to run the government themselves. So they asked Napoleon – by now, France's most famous soldier – to back them. With the army on their side, they believed they could govern France. But events did not turn out as they had planned.

1 Why did the Terror happen?

2 Why did it stop after the death of Robespierre?

3 Why do you think the new government banned the word 'revolutionary?'

4 Do you think that the Directory's policy of war against foreigners was likely to work?

'A better 'organised' constitution has never yet been organised by human wisdom.'

SOURCE 53
Sarcastic comment about the Directory by the revolutionary politician, Tom Paine.

SOURCE 54
The battle of Rivoli, 1797, painted by Felix Philippoteau (1814–1880). He was not born when the battle took place, but painted this picture many years later.

Napoleon

AIMS

In this unit, we shall look at the situation in France in 1799, ten years after the start of the Revolution. We will see who had gained, and who had lost, as a result of the revolutionary changes.

Next, we will look at the fascinating life story of Napoleon Bonaparte. He rose from humble beginnings as a young army officer to become Emperor of France. At the peak of his career it seemed that he would soon be master of all Europe too.

France in 1799

On 10 November, 1799 (19 Brumaire by the Revolutionary Calendar) there was uproar in the hall where members of the French government were meeting. After furious arguments, soldiers hustled many politicians out of the building, at bayonet-point (see Source 1). The troops were loyal to a young man called Napoleon Bonaparte, commander-in-chief of the army in Paris. A few weeks later, the Assembly was dissolved and a new government was installed, with Napoleon as leader. Suddenly, the Revolution was over. Why, and how, had this happened?

To answer this question, we need to look at France in 1799. How had the nation and its people been affected by ten years of revolutionary rule? Were the people really happier than they had been before the Revolution began? We also need to look at how rival groups of politicians felt in 1799, and why, once again, there were calls for the government to change.

Changes 1789 to 1799

SOURCE 1
Napoleon seizes power, November 1799. A painting by François Bouchot (1800–1842).

The State

- No longer any king or royal family, ruling by inherited power. Now politicians are in control of France. They claim to rule 'for the people' but squabble among themselves.

- Government (a national assembly) chosen by the people – all men can vote. But between 1789 and 1799 many people were too frightened or confused to vote. Different groups of politicians seized control of the assembly at different times.

- Laws are made by a national assembly, not by the king or his ministers. Powers of local *parlements* have been abolished.

- Old privileges (belonging to the king and the nobles) have also been abolished. Everyone is now equal in the eyes of the law.

The Economy

- Seriously weakened by the Revolution.

SOURCE 2
Bordeaux harbour – the Revolution disrupted trade and industry and caused problems for commercial cities such as this.

Cost of living:
This rose by 400 per cent between 1789 and 1797. Wages did not rise as quickly and many people went hungry.

Trade:
Overseas trade – the most profitable business before the Revolution (see Source 2) – now made up only 7 per cent of the French economy, instead of 25 per cent. Merchants and shopkeepers grew poorer.

Unemployment:
Rose rapidly; for example, in Bayeux, in 1787, the nobles and clergy employed 467 servants; in 1796 they employed 76. In Lyon, 50 per cent of the silk workshops closed down between 1789 and 1799.

Education

- Revolutionary governments planned to provide state education for everyone, but schools were never set up.

- Education was no longer to be controlled by the Roman Catholic Church.

- 50,000 pupils were attending colleges in 1789. Only 12,000 or 14,000 were attending central schools 10 years later. Basic literacy in France fell from 37 per cent in 1789 to around 30 per cent in 1815.

The Church

'We see lawful ministers, . . . exiled from their homeland . . . separated from their flocks. (We see) . . . monks hounded out; holy virgins (nuns) without refuge; colleges and schools without the resources to live; churches . . . dirty and in ruins . . . in a word, a soulless, bloodless, powerless skeleton.'

SOURCE 3
Comment by an Italian church official, looking back in 1802.

- Church no longer a major property-owner. Church lands had been sold to raise money for the state.

- Tithes (tax to support the church) abolished. Church expenses and priests' wages now paid by the state.

- Bishops and other senior church officials now appointed by the state, not by the Pope.

- Freedom of religion – people were not penalised any more if they were not Roman Catholic.

- Church now has no money to give as charity. Before the Revolution it provided money, schools and hospitals for poor people.

The people

Who lost and who gained as a result of the French Revolution? The answers to this question might surprise you.

Nobles
Losses:

The nobility lost their titles and their old privileges. A few also had their property destroyed in the Revolution (see Source 4). Others left their estates and fled abroad.

Gains:

Most nobles stayed in France and some played an important part in Revolutionary politics. Many profited from the Revolution. They enlarged their estates by purchasing lands which had belonged to the Church and were then taken over and sold by the State. Some nobles were given jobs by the government.

SOURCE 5
The Revolution did not change agriculture. Peasants still farmed in old-fashioned ways and were very poor.

SOURCE 4
Peasants attack nobles' estates, 1789.

ACTIVITY

'A strong leader is a good leader'.
Discuss this statement in a small group. Think of other examples of leaders in the past that you know of. Share your group's view with the rest of your class.

The bourgeoisie
Losses:

Some bourgeois lost their places in the old *parlements*. Some lost money because their wages did not keep pace with rising food prices.

Gains:

Wealthy bourgeois were able to purchase Church lands. Those who were educated as well as wealthy were given new jobs in state administration. Many members of the bourgeoisie – rich and poor – played an important part in Revolutionary politics.

Peasants
Losses:

Most poor people were poorer than before (see Source 5), because they no longer received charity from the church. In many parts of France new taxes were higher than pre-revolutionary ones, so peasants were worse off. Their wages did not keep pace with rising prices, so many went hungry. Men were forced to join the army and thousands were killed in battle.

Gains:

Feudal privileges were abolished, but this did not make very much difference politically or economically. Many peasants could vote.

'The Revolutionaries have killed our king, driven away our priests and sold all the goods that belonged to our churches. They have eaten all our food, and now they want our bodies, too . . . They won't get them.'

SOURCE 8
Comment by anti-revolutionary peasant from the Vendée district of western France.

SOURCE 6
Popular print showing a revolutionary citizen, encouraged by his wife and family, setting off to join the army.

'The young men shall go to battle; husbands shall make and transport provisions; women shall sew (soldiers') clothes and tents, and serve in the hospitals; children shall turn old linen into bandages, and old men shall go out into the public squares to rouse the courage of the fighters, and to preach the unity of the republic and the hatred of kings.'

SOURCE 7
The duties of French citizens in wartime, set out in a revolutionary decree (order) of 1793.

Civil Rights

The events of the Revolution also brought greater freedom to women and non-Catholics though it did not make them more prosperous. Protestants and Jews could now worship freely. New laws on marriage and divorce were passed which meant that women now had greater control over this important area of their lives.

France in crisis again?

The situation in 1799 reminded many French people of the crisis that had led to the Revolution breaking out in 1789. Prices were high, and many people could not afford to buy food. Peasants were rioting. The government was in debt, and the nation's leaders did not know how to solve France's economic problems. In Italy, the army was facing defeat. In Paris, politicians were divided into rival factions.

Takeover

When the republicans invited Napoleon to support their plans, they did not think that he would get involved in day-to-day politics. They assumed he would concentrate on the army, and on his military career. Instead, he seized complete control. In the rest of this unit we will look at how Napoleon ruled France. But first we must look at the army that helped him rise to power.

The people's army

In 1799, France was at war with almost all of Europe. For the first time, France was fighting with a 'citizen army'. At first, many French men and women were eager to fight for their country and the Revolution (see Source 6). But, as we can see from Source 7, warfare required an enormous effort and led to the sacrifice of hundreds of thousands of lives. It is not surprising that more and more ordinary men and women came to agree with the peasant quoted in Source 8.

---

1 Why did the French people welcome Napoleon?

2 Which group of people was likely to welcome him most?

Napoleon's rise to power

Napoleon Bonaparte was born on the Mediterranean island of Corsica in 1769. For centuries, Corsica had been ruled by Italy. It was sold to France in 1768. Napoleon's family was poor, but ranked as nobility. It was active in local politics, and in the Corsican nationalist movement that grew up after France took over.

Having noble blood qualified Napoleon to enter an exclusive boarding school at Brienne, in France, when he was nine years old. He then trained at a leading army college in Paris. He studied hard and got good reports. However, there was nothing in Napoleon's family background or his schooling to suggest the enormous impact that he would later have on France, and on the whole of Europe.

Historians have described Napoleon's career as a 'thunderbolt' or a 'shooting star', because of his sudden and dramatic success. He ended the Revolution, and took control of the government, in an amazingly short time. On these two pages, you can see some of the stages in his astonishing rise to power. In the rest of this unit, you can see what Napoleon did when he ruled France.

SOURCE 9
Napoleon crossing the Alps', a painting of Napoleon as a young man by David.

As a reward for his bravery, Napoleon is promoted. He is made commander of the army in Italy, where French armies are facing defeat. This is a great opportunity.

SOURCE 11
Josephine Beauharnais, a nobleman's widow. Napoleon married her in 1796.

On campaign in Italy, Napoleon soon wins brilliant victories, even though his troops are ragged and poorly-trained. He conquers Savoy, Milan and Mantua in 1796-97.

He prefers study to any kind of conversation, and nourishes his mind on good authors. He is moody, overbearing, self-centred. Though he speaks little, his replies are decisive and to the point . . . (He has) much self-love and boundless ambition.

SOURCE 10
Napoleon's report from army cadet school.

In 1791, Napoleon joins the Jacobin club. He eagerly supports its plans for reform. But after Robespierre's execution, all Jacobins are suspected, and the army commanders ask, is Napoleon really loyal? For a short time, he is imprisoned, but is soon set free. In October 1795, Napoleon proves his loyalty by helping to command the Parisian troops which put down the royalist rebellion of 13 Vendémiaire.

Soldiers, you are naked (and) badly fed . . . Rich provinces and great towns will be in your power, and in them you will find honour, glory, wealth, Soldiers of (France in) Italy, will you be wanting in courage and steadfastness?

SOURCE 12
Napoleon's announcement to his troops, 1796.

Napoleon becomes a hero in France. The Directory is grateful to him for restoring French confidence. However, a few politicians remember Robespierre:

'Be on the lookout against the leaders of the army . . . a strong citizen might one day take over, and run the government.'

SOURCE 14
Remark by Robespierre, made early in the Revolution.

SOURCE 15
The coup d'état of November 1799, when Napoleon seized power.

After taking control of northern Italy, Napoleon and his troops advance on the Austrian capital of Vienna. The Austrians are forced to agree to a humiliating peace treaty at Campo Formio in 1797.

SOURCE 13
British cartoon showing Napoleon and his troops looting art treasures from wealthy homes in Italy, 1796.

Napoleon – and the Directory – have great ambitions. If they can conquer Italy, why not advance further east, and win control of the entire Mediterranean sea? In 1798, Napoleon sets sail for Egypt. The same year, he wins an impressive victory against the Egyptians at the Battle of the Pyramids. But soon after, his fleet is destroyed by the British at the Battle of the Nile.

Inspired by the hope of winning further glory, Napoleon invades Syria in 1798 and 1799.

At home in France, Napoleon finds the country in crisis. The economy is in a mess, and people are discontented. The Directory seems powerless to help. On 19 Brumaire, with the help of his brother Lucien, he seizes power in a COUP D'ETAT.

There is bad news from home. Napoleon hears that his wife, Josephine (who was feeling neglected while he was away) is having an affair with a young army officer. Worse still, the French army has been badly defeated by Russian troops in Italy, and the Austrians are planning an attack. In October 1799, Napoleon hurries back to France.

SOURCE 16
Napoleon as First Consul, 1799, painted by Baron Gros (1771–1835).

Rebuilding France

Napoleon was appointed First Consul (out of three) in 1799 (see Source 16). Although the three Consuls were meant to share power, it was obvious from the start that he was the real leader. Like the revolutionary governments before them, the Consuls summoned National Assemblies to share in government. But, unlike the revolutionary assemblies, they had no power. Napoleon kept all that for himself.

Strong government

Napoleon had clear ideas about what he wanted for France. At home, he aimed for strong government and an end to the uncertainties of the revolutionary years. However, there was a price to pay for this: Napoleon didn't like being criticised. He shut down newspapers that disagreed with him.

'I want peace, as much to settle the present French government, as to save the world from chaos.'

SOURCE 17
Comment by Napoleon to a Prussian diplomat, 1800.

Old ideas

In 1800, Napoleon and his officials introduced a new constitution, or statement of how France should be governed. His first aim was peace (see Source 17). He needed to end the revolutionary wars so that there would be time and money for rebuilding France. Napoleon's constitution announced that the Revolution was over, but it did maintain a few revolutionary policies. It was anti-royal, and it kept the state separate from the Church. However, Napoleon did not want Church and state to be at war, as they had been in revolutionary times. In 1802 he signed a CONCORDAT (agreement) with the Pope.

SOURCE 18
The new law-code, introduced by Napoleon in 1804.

1 Why did Napoleon reorganise French local government? Give at least two reasons.

2 Which of Napoleon's reforms do you think was most important? Explain your answer.

3 Some of Napoleon's new laws seemed necessary. Some were a result of his own views and political opinions about things. Give an example of each.

New institutions

Most historians agree that Napoleon's greatest achievement was the way in which he re-built the French government administration. Within a surprisingly short time, he introduced many changes. Some of the most important were:

- a new system of laws, the Code Napoleon (see Source 18).

- new state-run schools and colleges which he hoped would train the most intelligent people for government service (see Source 19).

- the first National Curriculum.

- 83 *préfets* were appointed – these were powerful officials chosen by, and obedient to, the central government (see Source 20). They were put in charge of *départements* (local government regions, rather like English counties), in place of pre-revolutionary *parlements* and other local courts.

- a centralised civil service.

- a new police network (complete with spies).

- a national bank.

- a special 'Legion of Honour' to reward people who had given outstanding service to France.

Without Napoleon's energy, enthusiasm and strong-arm tactics (he imprisoned over 2,500 opponents without trial), none of this would have happened.

SOURCE 20
Nineteenth century painting, showing a *préfet* wearing the special uniform designed when Napoleon was in power.

> Be honest and hard-working girls, tender and modest wives and wise mothers, and you will be good patriots. True patriotism consists in fulfilling one's duties and valuing only rights appropriate to each according to sex and age, and not wearing the cap of liberty and pantaloons and not carrying a pike and pistol. Leave those to men who are born to protect you and make you happy.

SOURCE 21
Advice to young girls written by a revolutionary journalist in 1793, and repeated by Napoleon.

Napoleon inherited many experimental reforms from the revolutionary period. He kept decimal coinage and metric weights and measures, but he abolished the revolutionary calendar. Some of Napoleon's new laws came from pre-revolutionary times. Although he promised never to bring back feudal privileges, he restored noble titles, and created many new titles himself. Like so many of his actions, this was carefully calculated to win political support.

Napoleon also abolished the revolutionary laws which gave greater freedom to women. Source 21 suggests that he saw 'liberated' women as a danger to political peace.

SOURCE 19
Pupils in a French lycée (secondary school) today.

Master of Europe

From his early years in the army, Napoleon made no secret of his ambition to reach the top. If this helped France that would be good, but personal success was his main aim.

Even Napoleon's friends and close colleagues were sometimes surprised at just how much power and glory he wanted. As First Consul, he was sole ruler of France, but that was not enough (see Source 22). In 1804 he crowned himself Emperor. The Pope was at the ceremony, to give his blessing, but Napoleon was careful to place the crown on his head with his own hands. He wanted to make it clear that he owed his new position as Emperor to his own achievements. Source 23 shows a picture of this ceremony, painted after the event.

Many citizens were shocked when Napoleon divorced his wife because she was too old to have children. He was desperate for a son to follow him as Emperor, and so, when he was 40, he married the 18-year-old Austrian princess, Marie-Louise (Source 24). He made his four brothers 'kings' of conquered lands, and himself King of Italy. His mother became 'Madame Mère', a respectful title rather like 'Queen Mother'. When Napoleon's new wife gave birth to a son in 1811, the baby was proclaimed King of Rome. Less than 25 years after the Revolution, France now had a new 'royal family'.

Ambitions abroad

An emperor has to have an empire – a vast territory – to rule, so Napoleon set about conquering one. His motives were not simply ambition and greed. He genuinely wanted to protect France from its enemies, and to win new riches to restore its economy shattered by the Revolution. You can see a map of Napoleon's wars on page 47. On page 46 are details of his most important battles.

Napoleon as general

Napoleon had first come to power through his military skills, and it seems clear that he was a brilliant war leader. He enjoyed war, and found it interesting. He knew how to inspire his soldiers, and make them fight well. Even Napoleon's enemies admired his skills (see Source 25).

SOURCE 23
Napoleon crowns himself Emperor of France on 2 December 1804. A propaganda painting by Jacques-Louis David, who did not witness the scene, but painted it according to Napoleon's instructions.

'When I see an empty throne, I feel an urge to sit on it.'

SOURCE 22
Remark made by Napoleon in the early years of his rule.

attainment target 3

1 What can you tell about Napoleon from Source 22?

2 What can you tell about Napoleon's personality from Sources 22, 23 and 25?

3 How useful is Source 23 for telling us about Napoleon's coronation?

4 Source 23 is not accurate – how could historians make use of it anyway?

SOURCE 24
Marie-Louise of Austria, Napoleon's second wife, with their child, the King of Rome (born 1811).

> 'I used to say of him that his presence on the (battle) field made the difference of forty thousand men.'

SOURCE 25
Comment by the great British military commander, the Duke of Wellington, Napoleon's enemy.

On the battlefield. Napoleon used traditional hand-to-hand fighting but with 'extras' – such as squads of sharpshooters who ran in front of his soldiers as they marched into battle, firing at the enemy before they were ready to fight back. He made quick decisions, and managed to get his troops quickly to the right place at the right time. He also made good use of cannon. These were deadly new weapons. Source 26 shows a typical Napoleonic battlefield at Eylau in 1807.

Child of the devil?

Napoleon was not always admired. Many people hated and feared him. They felt that while he lived, there would never be peace in Europe. Even his generals were revolted by his cold-blooded attitude to warfare. He enjoyed the sight of a battlefield littered with bodies and once said, 'The corpse of a dead enemy always smells good.' In France, there were plots to assassinate him in 1800, 1804 and 1812. Source 27 shows a cartoon, produced by his enemies, suggesting that Napoleon's behaviour was so 'inhuman' that he could only have learned it from the devil.

SOURCE 27
Popular cartoon, showing Napoleon as the devil's child. Contrast this with Source 24.

SOURCE 26
Napoleon on the battlefield of Eylau, 1807.

Napoleon's wars 1804–1814

As we saw on pages 40–41, Napoleon had achieved great success leading French troops to victory in Italy. He had also used French military strength to negotiate a treaty at Campo Formio, in 1797, with Austria, France's powerful enemy. Now, in 1804, as Emperor of France, he planned once again to lead a French *Grande Armée* in battle against the great nations of Europe. Did he perhaps dream of one day becoming Emperor of Europe, as well? His most famous battles were:

1

Marengo 1805

176,000 French troops defeated Austrians and regained control of northern Italy. Napoleon almost lost this battle. If he had done, he might not have aimed to become Emperor of Europe.

2

Ulm 1805

French invasion force of almost 180,000, heading for Austria, defeated the Austrian army (33,000 men) at Ulm – the 'easiest victory'. Napoleon marches on.

3

Austerlitz 1805

Austrians re-gathered, and were supported by Russian allies, a total of 82,000 men. Napoleon and his soldiers advanced towards the Austrian capital. The two sides met; although the French army was smaller – around 65,000 – Austria and Russia were crushingly defeated. 20,000 men were killed or seriously wounded, and 15,000 were captured. France took over many countries ruled by Austria, including Belgium and the Netherlands.

4

Jena 1806

Prussia disliked Napoleon. Demanded that French troops, which had been occupying nearby German-speaking lands since the battle of Ulm, were withdrawn. In return, Napoleon declared war. The two sides met at Jena. Prussia was defeated. France took over many Prussian lands. A second battle was fought soon afterwards, at Auerstadt. 45,000 Prussian troops were scattered by a French army of only 26,000 men. In a single day, Napoleon had defeated Europe's most powerful kingdom.

5

Friedland 1807

Russian troops advanced towards France, through Poland. Napoleon hurried to attack. After fighting one battle against 80,000 Russians (at Eylau) in a snowstorm, his men faced a second Russian force. By a clever manoeuvre, Napoleon won victory. The Russians were massacred. 15,000 French were also killed. Napoleon then met the Russian Tsar Alexander, to discuss peace. They agreed the Treaty of Tilsit later in 1807.

6

Wagram 1810

Fought during Napoleon's second invasion of Austria. After a French defeat six weeks earlier at Aspern, near Vienna, Napoleon decided that he had to demonstrate new strength. He ordered the entire French army to march to Austria. Sheer weight of numbers (187,000 men and 500 cannon) caused the Austrians to retreat. As one historian has written, Wagram 'impressed Europe more than any earlier battle. Where previously there had been the hope that, with improved generalship and a bit of luck, Napoleon could be beaten, now it seemed as if his energy, his ruthlessness and his big battalions would carry him over any obstacle.'

7

Borodino 1812

Tsar Alexander of Russia wanted to trade peacefully with Britain. Napoleon wanted to stop this friendship between enemies of France, so he invaded Russia. At first, things went well. His army of 150,000 crushed the Russians at Borodino, although over a quarter (40,000) of his men were killed. Napoleon set off for Moscow but disaster struck. You can read more about Napoleon's Russian campaign on pages 50 and 51.

8

Leipzig 1813

Called the 'Battle of the Nations' because almost all Napoleon's enemies – Austria, Prussia, Russia, Britain, Sweden – joined together in a vast army (200,000 men) to fight him. They won. It showed, for the first time, that Napoleon could be defeated. It marked the beginning of the end of Napoleon's power.

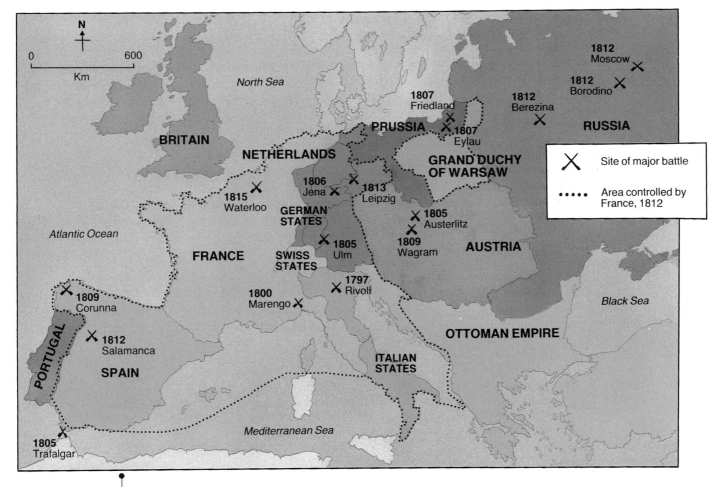

SOURCE 28
The locations of Napoleon's major battles.

Rival powers in Napoleon's Europe

France

Ruled by Napoleon. After 1807, he controlled most of Europe. Made marriage alliance (1810) with former major enemy, Austria. Considering plans to invade the Middle East. Facing GUERRILLA rebels in Spain (see page 49) and hostility from Britain.

Austria, Prussia (north Germany), Russia

The largest and most powerful states in Eastern Europe. Napoleon's enemies, for most of his time in power. Previously, they had been at war with Revolutionary France. All defeated by Napoleon in battle. All forced to give up large areas of land. They feared that all Europe would soon be ruled by Napoleon and his family – he made his brothers and sister rulers of their newly-conquered lands.

Germany and Italy

Not the same as present-day countries with the same name. Before Napoleon, ruled by many independent princes and controlled by (or allied to) Austria, Prussia and Russia. Invaded by Napoleon's armies and, after 1807, controlled by France. Men from conquered lands were forced to fight in the French army. They hated this.

Great Britain

Had been at war with France for much of the 18th century. Like Austria, Prussia and Russia, opposed Revolutionary ideas. Now was preparing to defend itself against invasion by Napoleon's troops (see pages 48 and 49).

Spain and Portugal

Allies of Britain. Invaded by France in 1807 (Portugal) and 1808 (Spain) (see page 49).

Old enemies

England and France had been enemies for many years before Napoleon came to power. At first, some British politicians and writers welcomed the French Revolution. However, most people in Britain were horrified by the execution of Louis XVI and by the violence and bloodshed during the Terror.

As Napoleon seized more and more power, British leaders began to think it was their duty to defend the world against him. Cartoons like Source 29 were published, to spread these views.

War at sea

In 1798, French troops led by Napoleon defeated British soldiers at Aboukir Bay, in Egypt. But a few weeks later, at the Battle of the Nile, English ships destroyed France's Mediterranean fleet, and wrecked Napoleon's bid to gain power in the Middle East.

War broke out once more in 1803, when Napoleon's troops occupied the Netherlands, Britain's ally. Soon afterwards, in 1804, Napoleon launched an invasion of Britain. This failed, because of bad weather, bad planning and bad luck. In 1805, the British navy, commanded by Nelson (see Source 30) hit back. They destroyed 20 French warships sailing off Cape Trafalgar (see Source 31) on the coast of Spain. Britain now controlled the seas all around France, and Napoleon never tried to fight at sea again.

SOURCE 29
Cartoon, showing Napoleon as a greedy spider, by the English artist Thomas Rowlandson (1756–1827).

SOURCE 30
Admiral Lord Nelson and his fellow navy commanders plan their battle against Napoleon on board ship.

SOURCE 31
The battle of Trafalgar, 1805.

SOURCE 32
Arthur Wellesly, Duke of Wellington (1769-1852).
(Painting by Goya).

attainment target 2

Here are three different descriptions of Napoleon, written by modern historians:

- 'a military genius'
- 'he was chiefly interested in power'
- '(his) violence . . . bred hatred and fear, and (his) trickery destroyed all trust'.

1 Which of these views do you think is more accurate? Explain your choice and compare it with the others.

2 Which sources in this unit would you use to support each of the views above?

SOURCE 33
Spanish guerrillas making bullets.

The 'Continental System'

After Trafalgar, Napoleon decided to use a different weapon against Britain. He forbade all French people – and people in all lands conquered by France – to buy British goods, or goods from British colonies. He hoped an 'economic war' would ruin the 'nation of shopkeepers', as he scornfully called Britain. He also hoped that this economic war – known as the 'Continental System' – would strengthen the French economy, as most of Europe would be forced to buy French goods instead.

His plan did not succeed. Smuggling was widespread and people in conquered lands did all they could to break the trading rules.

The Peninsular War

Britain and France were soon fighting again. After Napoleon's troops invaded Portugal in 1807 and Spain in 1808, these two countries (known as the Iberian Peninsula) became a battleground. The Spanish people rebelled against French government, and asked Britain to help them fight.

Britain sent rather rough and ready troops, but they were led by two brilliant generals: Arthur Wellesley (later Duke of Wellington, shown in Source 32) and Sir John Moore.

The rugged Spanish landscape, and the TERRORIST tactics used by Spanish freedom fighters meant that, for once, Napoleon could not win. The freedom fighters were known as guerrillas (see Source 33). They would not give in even when French soldiers used brutal punishments. After Britain won important battles at Corunna in 1809 and at Salamanca in 1812, the French had to retreat. The Peninsula was free.

A fatal mistake

In 1810, France controlled almost all of Europe. Only Britain, Russia and Spain remained free. In 1810, Tsar Alexander, shown in Source 34, announced that he was going to ignore Napoleon's 'Continental System' and start trading with Britain again. Napoleon was angry and alarmed. If Britain and Russia became friends, they could defeat France (see Source 35).

Napoleon decided to invade Russia. He planned to give the Tsar a 'short, sharp shock', by attacking Russia with an enormous army, winning a few quick victories, and then marching home. Napoleon hoped he would be able to force the Tsar to abandon his friendship with Britain. Then France would be supreme.

SOURCE 34
Tsar Alexander of Russia (1777–1825).

SOURCE 35
British cartoon, glorifying Russian strength.

1 List two short-term and two long-term consequences of Napoleon's attack on Russia.

2 What do you think might have happened if Napoleon had invaded Russia in summertime?

3 What does Napoleon's Russian campaign tell us about (a) his character? (b) his attitude towards his soldiers? (c) his political ambitions?

SOURCE 36
Napoleon's Russian campaign, 1812.

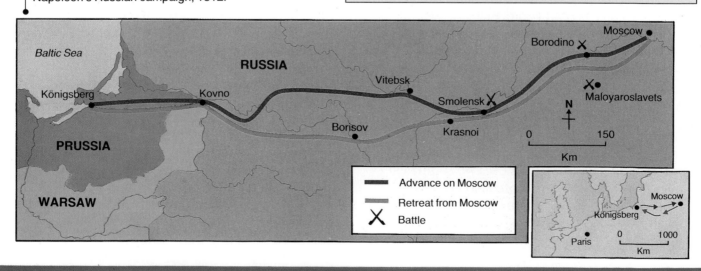

A massive attack

Napoleon's plans went disastrously wrong. In 1812, he assembled a vast army on the border between Poland and Russia. He hoped to overpower the Russians by sheer weight of numbers. But the Russians refused to fight. Instead, they retreated towards Moscow, their capital city. Napoleon's troops were forced to chase them through harsh, hostile territory (the route of their long journey is shown in Source 36). Food ran short; Napoleon hoped for a brief campaign, so he had only arranged supplies for three weeks. The two sides fought at Borodino, about 110 kilometres from Moscow. The French won the battle, but the Russians would not admit defeat. Napoleon led his armies onwards to Moscow, and set fire to the city (Source 37). But Tsar Alexander still would not surrender; he knew that, in spite of their seeming success, Napoleon and his men were trapped.

Failure

Napoleon was forced to abandon his attack on Moscow in October 1812. His men were exhausted, cold and hungry (see Source 38). The bitter Russian winter was just beginning – soon, heavy snow would fall, and the temperature would remain below freezing point all day long. He was 4,000 kilometres from Paris, and surrounded by enemies. He had stopped trying to make Tsar Alexander give in. Now his task was to try to get his men home.

SOURCE 37
Moscow in flames, after being attacked by Napoleon's troops.

'General Winter'

Napoleon was defeated by the problems of moving an army vast distances across Russian territory, and, most of all, by the Russian weather. 'General Winter' had succeeded where human army commanders had failed. 'He' had conquered Napoleon (see Source 39). Europe's mightiest army perished from cold, hunger and disease.

At home in France, people were horrified. They mourned the dead soldiers and plotted to remove Napoleon from power. News of the disastrous retreat from Moscow echoed all round Europe. The invasion of Russia had been a fatal mistake. Napoleon's army lost 570,000 men there as well as 200,000 horses and 1,100 cannon. People began to say that the French empire – and its Emperor – were not so great as they appeared.

SOURCE 38
French soldiers suffered terribly on the retreat from Moscow in the winter of 1812–1813.

'Russia has two generals she can trust – Generals January and February.'

SOURCE 39
Remark made by Tsar Nicholas I, who ruled Russia later in the 19th century, looking back at 1813.

From hero to villain

SOURCE 40
Napoleon in imperial robes, painted by Francois-Pascal Gérard.

SOURCE 41
Napoleon faces death at the battle of Leipzig. A British cartoon of 1813.

ACTIVITY

Make a wall display on the topic of 'heroes', from the present-day and from the past. Write captions to explain why you have chosen each man or woman.

Sources 40 and 41 present two contrasting images of Napoleon. Source 40 shows a picture of him as Emperor which he ordered to be painted when he was at the height of his power. Source 41 shows a cartoon of Napoleon drawn by a British artist in 1813. As Napoleon himself said, 'From the sublime to the ridiculous. There is only one step.'

The cartoon in Source 41 was published after Napoleon had been crushingly defeated at Leipzig by an alliance of his enemies. In 1814, France faced invading armies sent from Britain, Austria and Prussia. Napoleon also faced enemies at home; Source 42 records just some of their complaints. Many French people felt that war was tragic even when they were victorious. Now they were defeated, the waste of lives and money seemed inexcusable.

> Our ills are at their height. The homeland is threatened at all points of the frontier; we are suffering from poverty and wretchedness unexampled in the whole history of the state. Commerce is destroyed, industry dying. . . What are the causes of these unspeakable miseries? A troublesome administration, too many taxes, dreadful methods adopted to collect them, and even crueller schemes to recruit the armies. . . A barbaric and endless war swallows up . . . youth torn from education, agriculture, commerce and the arts. . .

SOURCE 42
Complaint by members of Napoleon's government, 1813.

Giving up power

In 1814, Paris was captured by allied troops. Napoleon now had no choice – he had to abdicate. Source 43 shows an emotional moment – Napoleon saying farewell to his army. The invading allies sent Napoleon into exile on the tiny Mediterranean island of Elba. He was given a royal title, but he no longer had any power. In future, the invaders decided, France was to be ruled once more by a king. They invited the oldest surviving brother of Louis XVI to reign. He took the title of Louis XVIII, and was crowned later that year.

Napoleon saying farewell to his troops, 1814.

'A battle of giants.'

SOURCE 44
Contemporary comment on the battle of Waterloo.

'The nearest-run thing you ever saw in your life.'

SOURCE 45
Comment by the Duke of Wellington, commander of the British army at the battle of Waterloo.

The 'hundred days'

Napoleon did not like life in exile. He plotted to seize power once more. In 1815, he escaped from Elba, and sailed to the south of France. He marched towards Paris, attracting eager followers along the way. They hoped he would bring back France's greatness. King Louis XVIII escaped to Belgium, in terror.

Back in control, in Paris, Napoleon promised peace. He said he would govern France gently, according to the law. He also said he had given up his plans to conquer the whole of Europe, but many people did not believe him. They watched suspiciously while he began to recruit a new army. Just two months after Napoleon arrived in Paris, he led 150,000 men to invade Belgium. There, he fought British and Prussian troops, led by Wellington and Blücher, Europe's two best generals, at the battle of Waterloo (see Sources 44, 45 and 46). He was only just defeated (see Source 45), but that was enough to end his second chance as Emperor after only a hundred days. Napoleon was exiled again, this time to St Helena, an island in the South Atlantic. He died there, six years later, aged 52.

SOURCE 46
The battlefield at Waterloo, in Belgium. Painted many years afterwards by Sir William Allen (1803–1852).

A new Europe

After Napoleon

In 1815, the nations that had joined together to defeat Napoleon (Austria, Russia, Prussia and Britain) held a meeting – the Congress of Vienna (see Source 1). Now that Napoleon was safely out of the way, they had to make sure that no single individual ever threatened the peace of Europe again.

Far away on the island of St Helena, Napoleon's new life was very different and he was feeling homesick. He was also trying to persuade himself – and others – that the French people missed him (see Source 2). The nations gathered at the Congress of Vienna were of a very different opinion. They did not want him back.

AIMS

In this Unit, we will look at what happened to France and to the rest of Europe after Napoleon was driven from power. We will look, too, at the influence of the Revolution and of Napoleon's empire on fashions in art, design and ideas. Finally, we will ask, 'what is a revolution?'

SOURCE 1
European government leaders meet at the Congress of Vienna, 1815.

SOURCE 2
Written by Napoleon while in exile on St Helena.

'Millions of men weep for us, the homeland (France) sighs . . . the wishes of the nations are for us.'

SOURCE 4
How Metternich's opponents described his new, backward-looking system of government.

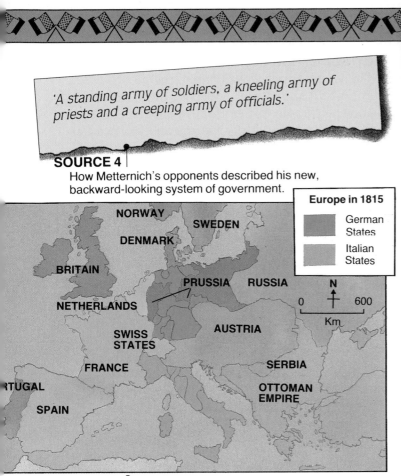

Europe in 1815

- German States
- Italian States

SOURCE 3
New boundaries for European states drawn up at the Congress of Vienna.

SOURCE 5
King Louis XVIII (1755–1824) in royal robes. A painting by Francois-Louis Gérard.

New boundaries

Lands conquered by Napoleon were shared out among the allies who had defeated him (see Source 3). Contemporaries said that 'the map of Europe is being re-drawn'. Germany, Italy and Scandinavia were divided up. Belgium was given to the Netherlands. This policy soon proved disastrous. No-one considered the views of the many different ethnic groups living in those countries. Years later, there were riots and revolutions as nationalist groups sought independence for their homelands.

1　Why do you think the political boundaries drawn up at the Congress of Vienna did not last?

2　When he was an old man, Prince Metternich said that all his life had been spent 'trying to support decaying structures'. What do you think he meant by this?

Return to the past

What kind of government did the allies want to replace Napoleon? Basically, they wanted a return to the days before the Revolution. This would mean rule by kings and princes, a powerful Church, a strong army and an efficient civil service, all loyal to the king and his ministers. Free discussion, democratic elections and 'the will of the people' would not be allowed. The diplomats who persuaded European leaders to go back to these old ways were led by the conservative Prince Metternich of Austria. He had always been an enemy of the French Revolution, but some people disagreed or were critical (see Source 4). To them it looked as if all Europe would be kept under tight government control.

A new king

The allies also decided that there should, once again, be a king of France. Louis XVI's brother, Louis-Stanislas-Xavier, was next in line to the throne. He had already been welcomed by French royalists as King Louis XVIII, and, at Vienna, the allies agreed that he should remain the ruler of France. You can see the new King's portrait, painted to proclaim his royal splendour to all Europe, in Source 5.

Heritage of the Revolution

After Napoleon was sent into exile, Louis XVIII ruled as King of France. He was old (nearly 60), unhealthy and not very intelligent. His comment in Source 6 reveals his political ambitions to 'turn back the clock' to pre-revolutionary days, and govern the country in the old style. He relied far too often on his favourites for advice. They were usually only thinking of themselves.

Peace

Understandably, this incompetent royal government led to crisis after crisis. There was one issue, however, on which Louis and his people were united. They wanted peace. Over 860,000 young French men (aged between 23 and 44) were killed in Napoleon's wars. Before that, another 40,000 French men and women had died during the Revolution. In towns, merchants and manufacturers wanted the chance to build new factories and re-establish trade. In the countryside, lawyers and estate-owners, noble families and peasants all wanted the chance to get on with their lives free from the threat of war. Source 7 shows the 'domestic' ideal; which many French families aimed for – tranquillity, comfort and content.

> 'Courtier: 'Sire, now you are King of France.'
> Louis XVIII: 'When have I NOT been King?'

SOURCE 6
Remark made by Louis XVIII, when a servant congratulated him in 1814.

Shaping society

The wish for peace was one of the most important short-term effects of the Revolution and the Napoleonic era for French society. But there were other, longer-term consequences, as well. Even though the monarchy was restored, almost all the old government institutions had been swept away. Many important new ones – such as the Revolution's local government and Napoleon's education system – were now shaping French society, as they still do today.

The French nation did not forget its revolutionary heritage. The streets of Paris were ornamented with grand monuments such as the Eiffel Tower (see Source 8), commemorating revolutionary events. In many other towns, streets were re-named after revolutionary heroes or Napoleon's great victories. Even the fighting words of the Marseillaise, the French national anthem, (see Source 9), still remind French people of their nation's revolutionary past.

attainment target 1

Compare life in France in 1788 (as described in Unit 1) with life in France in 1820. Look at the changes affecting all the different groups in French society – the royal family, the nobles, the clergy, the bourgeois and the peasants.

1 Whose life had changed the most?

2 Whose life had changed for the better and whose for the worse?

SOURCE 7
Mid-19th century painting of a comfortable bourgeois family in France. After the Revolution and Napoleon's reign many people hoped for peace and a quiet life at home.

Symbols of liberty

During the 19th century, there were several rebellions by the French people against governments which they believed to be unjust. In 1830, King Charles X, Louis XVI's youngest brother, was driven into exile. In 1848, a revolutionary commune ran Paris, turning another king, Louis-Philippe, off the throne. In all these upheavals, protesters were inspired by the 1789 Revolution. Romantic images of republican ideas, such as 'Liberty' were popular (see Source 10). The artists who painted romantic pictures hoped they would link all these later rebellions with the original Revolution, forming a 'Great Tradition' of revolutionary thought and action, and glorifying France.

> The bloody flag of tyrannical government still waves above our heads. Can you hear, throughout the land, the shouts of the soldiers? Citizens, get your weapons! Organise your troops! March onwards, onwards! Let the poisoned blood of our enemies soak into our fields.

SOURCE 9
The first verse of the Marseillaise (translated).

SOURCE 10
Painting by Eugène Delacroix (1798–1863) called 'Liberty Leading the People'.

Revolutions round the world

The words in Source 11 were spoken by Gabriel Noel, a volunteer soldier in the revolutionary army, in 1792. Many French people, from wealthy deputies to poor citizens of Paris, shared Noel's hopes. They believed that revolutionary France was leading the way towards a new and better society, where freedom and equality would be guaranteed for all.

The French Revolution and the years when Napoleon ruled, certainly did affect Europe, and, gradually, the rest of the world. You can see a timeline of revolutions since 1789 on page 60. These revolutions were inspired by French ideas of liberty and equality. They were also caused by a new, powerful spirit of NATIONALISM (national pride and demands for independence). This grew as a reaction partly to Napoleon's plans for French conquests, and partly to the new national boundaries insensitively imposed at the Congress of Vienna.

'The spirit of liberty is going to envelop the entire world.'

SOURCE 11
Comment by a French revolutionary soldier, 1792.

SOURCE 12
A soldier from the French National Guard and a woman wearing a coat designed in military style.

SOURCE 13
Empress Josephine (Napoleon's wife) wearing (Roman) Empire style clothes, painted by David.

Revolutionary style

But the French Revolution had other, more surprising, effects. It caused major changes in the world of art, fashion and design. Artists who sympathised with revolutionary ideas produced dramatic paintings – often vast in size – designed to glorify the people and events shown in them. The best-known of these artists was Jacques-Louis David (1748–1825). You can see examples of his work on pages 40, 44 and above.

Source 12 reveals that, at first, clothing styles for both men and women copied details from military uniforms worn by French soldiers. It was fashionable to look (slightly) revolutionary – it showed you were in touch with the latest events, even if you did not share revolutionary political ideas.

SOURCE 14
Afternoon dress from Heideloff's 'Gallery of Fashion' 1794–1800 inspired by Josephine's Empire style.

SOURCE 15
An Empire-style house interior. The entrance hall of a stately home at Tulgen in Sweden.

The Roman ideal

Source 13 shows a change of mood – Josephine's loose, simple frock is copied from ancient Roman designs. It reflects new ideas among revolutionary politicians. When France became a republic, politicians looked back to Republican Rome as a model of what their new state might be. Men gave themselves Roman names, like 'Gracchus', while women wore Roman clothes.

Napoleon also liked to think of himself as a modern-day Roman emperor, so Roman styles stayed in fashion while he ruled France. You can see examples of so-called 'Empire' clothing and room decoration in Sources 14 and 15.

New ideas

Though many people at first supported the ideals of the French Revolution, they were horrified by the execution of the King, and the violence of the Terror. They soon came to distrust Napoleon, too. The comments in Sources 16 and 17 are from poems written by two of Europe's most influential thinkers. They tell us that revolutionary ideas were no longer in fashion. A new way of looking at the world, and at politics, would shortly take their place.

Revolutionary inspiration

The French Revolution was just one of many Revolutions that took place between 1750 and 1850 (see page 60). Revolutionary politicians did not all share the same aims as revolutionary leaders in France. Even so, the French Revolution continued to inspire people in many parts of the world. It showed that if ordinary citizens were prepared to take action, they could transform their nations and their lives.

'. . . I wish men to be free
As much from mobs as kings . . .'

SOURCE 16
From the poem *Don Juan* by the British poet Lord Byron, written between 1818 and 1823.

'The world is weary of the past
Oh, might it die or rest at last'

SOURCE 17
From the poem *Hellas* written by another British poet, Percy Bysshe Shelley in 1820.

Revolutions

1 How can we evaluate the effects of (i) the French Revolution (ii) Napoleon's Empire:
a Who did they help?
b Was all the bloodshed justified?
c Did they change France only in the short term?
d Or did they change France forever?

2 Ever since 1789, politicians such as the Russian leader, Lenin, have been inspired by the Revolution's ideas of freedom and equality. Political propaganda – words and images – about revolutionary leaders have been important as well. Compare the picture of Lenin (Source 18), with the portrait of Napoleon (Source 9, page 40).

a Why do you think Napoleon asked to be portrayed in that dramatic pose?

b Why do you think Russian artists designed Lenin's picture as they did?

ACTIVITY

The timeline opposite shows there have been many different revolutions since 1789.
1 As a class project, arrange a display describing all the revolutions you can find out about that have happened in the past 10 years, together with their causes and their results. How do they compare with the French Revolution?
2 Can you also think of 'revolutions' in fashion, sport, music, technology or ideas?
3 Finish this sentence: 'A revolution is a time when . . .'

SOURCE 18
A Russian revolutionary poster, showing the Communist leader, Lenin, painted 1917-1920.

Revolutions 1750-1850

Date	Place	Aims
1755	Corsica	Independence
1768	Geneva	Democracy
1773	South-east Russia	Independence
1775	America	Independence and democracy
1789	**France**	**Liberty and equality**
1789	Liège (Belgium)	Anti-feudalism
1790	Hungary	Independence
1791	Haiti	Anti-slavery
1791	Poland	Democracy and freedom
1793	Sardinia	Independence
1798	Ireland	Independence and religious freedom
1804	Serbia	Independence
1808	Spain	Anti-Napoleon/ Independence
1809	Austrian Tyrol	Anti-Napoleon/ Independence
1811- 1829	Central and South America	Independence
1830	Greece	Independence
1830	Belgium	Independence
1831	Poland	Independence
1848- 1849	Italy Germany Hungary	Independence

1 Why do you think so many later revolutions were inspired by the French Revolution?

2 Look at the examples of paintings by David mentioned in the text on page 58. How does he glorify the people and events he is portraying in his paintings?

Glossary

Anarchy
Without government or laws.

Ancestors
People from whom we are descended; our parents, grandparents, great-grandparents, etc.

Assignats
Certificates issued by the revolutionary government in France, which came to be used as a form of paper money.

Bourgeois
Living in a town.

Bourgeoisie
People who lived in towns; an important group in French society.

Cahiers
Literally, notebooks; used to describe the lists of complaints made by people living in the provinces. They were discussed at the first meeting of the Estates-General.

Capitation
Poll-tax.

Consul
A title for a leader of a republican government. It originated in Ancient Rome.

Continental System
Napoleon's scheme to try and make all France and all lands conquered by France boycott British-made goods. It failed.

Coup d'État
A sudden change of government, usually the result of force.

Départements
Local government regions, rather like British counties. France was first divided into départements by the revolutionary government in 1791.

Deputies
Elected representatives, rather like Members of Parliament, who played an important part in the revolutionary government.

Directory
The group of moderate politicians who governed France after the Terror ended in 1794. They were driven out of office when Napoleon seized power in 1799.

Divine Right
The belief that kings or other heads of state are appointed by God. Usually believed only by kings, their ministers and leading church authorities. According to this belief, any criticism or rebellion might be viewed as a sin (since it went against God's choice) as well as a political crime.

Douanes
Customs duties paid on goods taken to market.

Feudalism
An ancient system of rights and privileges connected with landholding. Under the feudal system, a major landowner had the right to demand rent plus various other money payments and sometimes also work from the peasants who lived on his or her land.

Feudal dues
Payments made to a landowner by peasants living on their land, in return for rights such as using the landowner's mill to grind their corn, or fishing in his rivers. They were deeply resented.

Gabelle
A tax on salt. Everyone had to pay this, since salt was used in cooking and for preserving food.

Galante
Elegant, graceful and light-hearted.

Girondins
A group of revolutionary politicians, with outspoken, but not extremist views. They quarrelled with the Jacobins over how much violence it was necessary to use against critics of the Revolution.

Guerrillas

Fighters who use surprise tactics, such as ambushes or hit-and-run raids, against their enemies, instead of fighting pitched battles.

Jacobins

A group of revolutionary politicians who believed that criticism of the Revolution was dangerous, and should be stopped by executing all opponents. They were responsible for 'The Terror' of 1793 to 1794.

Imperial

Belonging to an empire.

Laboureurs

Peasants who were rich enough to own their own land.

Lycée

Secondary school, which aimed to produce academically very successful pupils with well-trained minds. French secondary schools are still called lycées.

Métayers

Peasants who rented land from people wealthier than themselves. In return, they gave the landowner half of the crops or livestock they produced.

Moderates

Politicians who supported the Revolution, but did not want to see major changes happen too quickly, or with too much bloodshed.

Nationalism

Loyalty to a country and its territory, language and way of life. Usually combined with a wish for political independence.

Préfets

Local government officials, each responsible for a département. Introduced by Napoleon.

Pre-revolutionary

Something that happened before the Revolution.

Radical

People who campaign for sweeping changes in politics and society. The word 'radical' comes from the Latin for 'root'; radical revolutionaries wanted to 'uproot' the French government and introduce something completely new.

Royalist

A supporter of King Louis XVI and his policies.

Salons

Drawing-rooms of large houses. The places where groups of politicians and their friends met to discuss current affairs and revolutionary ideas.

Sans-culottes

Ordinary, working men and women (and their supporters from other groups in French society) who played an important part in revolutionary politics. Their views were radical.

Taille personelle

A yearly tax on personal possessions, paid to the pre-revolutionary government.

Terrorist

Someone who uses violence – often against civilians – to fight for their political beliefs.

Title

A tax of one-tenth of produce, paid yearly to the Church.

Tribunal

A kind of court; the revolutionary tribunals had power to sentence people to death.

Vingtième

A tax of one-twentieth of the value of land, paid yearly to the pre-revolutionary government.

Index

Page numbers in **bold** refer to illustrations/captions

First published 1994 by Collins Educational
77-85 Fulham Palace Road
Hammersmith
London W6 8JB

ISBN 0 00 327260 5

Cover design by Glynis Edwards
Book designed by Glynis Edwards and Derek Lee
Series planned by Nicole Lagneau
Edited by Louise Wilson
Picture research by Suzanne Williams
Artwork by Julia Osorno
Production by Mandy Inness

Typeset by Dorchester Typesetting Group Ltd

Printed and bound in Hong Kong

Acknowledgements

Every effort has been made to contact the holders of
copyright material but if any have been inadvertently
overlooked, the publishers will be pleased to make the
necessary arrangements at the first opportunity.

Photographs The publishers would like to thank the
following for permission to reproduce photographs on
these pages:

T = top, B = bottom, R = right, C = centre, L = left

The Bowes Museum, Barnard Castle, Co. Durham
25R; Bibliothèque Nationale, Paris 42B, 43T; The
Bridgeman Art Library/Lauros-Giraudon 7B, 8R, 10T,
10B, 11B, 12BL, 20R, 21T & B, 22B, 23T, 25L, 26B,
29TL, 31R & L, 32R, 35B, 36, 39, 40L & R, 41T, 42T,
44, 45T, 42BL, 48TL, 52T, 53T, 55, 56, 57B, 58L; The
Bridgeman Art Library/Victoria & Albert Museum,
London 53B; The Bridgeman Art Library/Yale
University Art Gallery, New Haven 13B; Bulloz/Musée
Carnavalet 9B; Bulloz/Bibliothèque Nationale, Paris
41B, 45BR; E.T. Archive 6R, 11T (Dulwich Picture
Gallery, London), 16, 17, 20L, 23B, 31B, 32L, 50L,
51R, 58R, 59L & R, 60; Fotomas Index 15R, 29B, 52B;
Robert Harding Picture Library 7T; Michael Holford
51L; The Hutchison Library/Tony Souter 57T; Impact
Photos/Eric Maulave/Cedri 43B; Lauros-Giraudon 15L,
19, 28B, 38T; Lauros-Giraudon/Musées de la Ville de
Paris 26T, 27B, 30, 33, 34B; Mansell Collection 29TR,
34R, 35T; Mary Evans Picture Library 12TR & BR;
Ampliaciones Reproducciones MAS, Barcelona 49R;
The National Gallery, London 49L; The Nelson
Museum, Monmouth 48TR; Musée d'Orange, photo
Bernard Delgado 14R; © Photothèque des Musées
Nationaux de la Ville de Paris by SPADEM 1993/
Musée Carnavalet 9B Debucourt, *Promenade au
Palais Royal*, 13T Anon, *Palais Royal, Caveau Café*,
22T Demarchy, *Demolition of the Cordeliers Church*;
© Photo Réunion des Musées Nationaux, Paris 8L (J.
B. Charpentier, *The Family of the Duke of Penthièvre*,
1768 Palace of Versailles) 37 J. Vernet, *The Port of
Bordeaux,* Musée de la Marine), 54 J. B. Isabey, *The
Congress of Vienna* 1815 Musée du Louvre);
Weidenfeld & Nicolson Archives 48B.

Cover photograph: The Bridgeman Art Library

The author and publishers gratefully acknowledge the
following publications from which written sources in
this book are drawn:

Oxford University Press for extracts from William
Doyle, the Oxford History of the French Revolution,
1989; Blackwell Publishers Ltd for extracts from JM
Thompson, English Eye Witnesses; Penguin Books
Ltd for extracts from Alfred Cobban, 'The History of
Modern France, Volumes I and II, JM and MJ Cohen,
Penguin Dictionary of Quotations, 1960 and C
MacEvedy, Penguin Atlas of Modern History; Collins
(now HarperCollins) for extracts from Peter Vansittart,
Voices of the Revolution, 1989.